D0899135

Regina Anderson Andrews
Harlem Renaissance Librarian

Regina Anderson Andrews

Harlem Renaissance Librarian

ETHELENE WHITMIRE

University of Illinois Press

URBANA, CHICAGO, AND SPRINGFIELD

Library of Congress Cataloging-in-Publication Data
Whitmire, Ethelene, 1968–
Regina Anderson Andrews, Harlem Renaissance
librarian / Ethelene Whitmire.
pages   cm
Includes bibliographical references and index.
ISBN 978-0-252-03850-1 (hardback : acid-free paper)
ISBN 978-0-252-09641-9 (ebook)
1. Andrews, Regina. 2. Library directors—United
States—Biography. 3. African American women
librarians—United States—Biography 4. New York
Public Library. 135th Street Branch—Biography.
5. Harlem Renaissance. 6. Harlem (New York,
N.Y.)—Intellectual life. 7. African Americans—
New York (State)—New York—Intellectual life. 8.
African American theater—New York (State)—New
York—History—20th century. 9. Discrimination in
employment.
I. Title.
Z720.A63W48   2014
025.1'97092—dc23   2013039074

In loving memory of my father, Dennis Johnnie Whitmire
For my mother, Valerie Irene Whitmire, who introduced
me to the wonderful world of libraries

Contents

Acknowledgments

I would like to especially thank Raquel Von Cogell and Dr. Cherene Sherrard-Johnson, who enthusiastically supported this project during the entire journey.

I began this journey as an assistant professor at University of California–Los Angeles (UCLA) Department of Information Studies. Crucial support came from Dean Aimee Doerr and the Graduate School of Education and Information Studies and from Chair Anne Gilliland and Professor Mary Niles Maack. Research funds supported Dalena Hunter, my former research assistant, who was there from the beginning. We traveled to Harlem for the first official research trip to the Schomburg Center for Research in Black Culture, where Steven Fullwood provided critical support. We stayed in a wonderful brownstone bed-and-breakfast decorated like the Harlem Renaissance period, which inspired the decoration of my home office for this project. Additional assistance was provided by Thomas Lannon and Laura Ruttum, from the Manuscripts and Archives division of the Stephen A. Schwarzman Building of the New York Public Library.

I received research support from several sources: The Gilder Lehrman Institute of American History's Scholarly Fellowship; the University of Wisconsin–Madison's Graduate School and the Vilas Associate Award; the University of Wisconsin–System's Institute for Race & Ethnicity grant; University of Wisconsin–Madison's Center for Research on Gender & Women's–Feminist Scholars Fellowship, which gave me an additional semester to write, along with the Faculty Sabbatical Leave Program for the entire 2009–2010 academic year.

I would like to thank the University of Illinois Press staff, especially my editor, Larin McLaughlin, and Dawn Durante and Roberta Spartenburg, who helped to bring this book into fruition. Both Nancy Albright and Karen Fein provided editorial assistance. I would also like to thank Kathleen Pfeiffer and the anonymous reader of this manuscript for the University of Illinois Press who provided critical and important feedback. David B. Gracy II, editor of *Libraries & the Cultural Record,* and anonymous readers provided feedback on the manuscript for an article, "Breaking the Color Barrier: Regina Andrews and the New York Public Library," which was later revised to become Chapter 6.

During research visits to the New York City area, I was provided support and nice meals from my family, including my sister, librarian Denise Whitmire O'Shea, brother-in-law, Neal O'Shea, and niece, Maura O'Shea; my brother Darren Whitmire; and especially my mother, Valerie Whitmire, who provided copious cups of coffee. My cousin Kevin Whitmire helped me search for Andrews's homes and workplaces in New York City. Dr. Furaha Norton drove me to Wilberforce University to see where Regina went to college, the dorm where she resided, and the Carnegie Library where she worked. Officer Herman B. Mann of Wilberforce was an excellent guide and university historian.

Members of my seminar section, seminar leader Susan Ware, and guest Nancy Hewitt, at the 2007 Radcliffe/Schlesinger Library's "Writing Past Lives: Biography as History" Seminar on Gender History, gave critical feedback during my presentation on what is now Chapter 5 about the Harlem Experimental Theatre. Nancy Beckett, instructor for the University of Wisconsin's Writers-By-The-Lake Creative Non-Fiction course, and my fellow students also provided important encouragement.

In my department at the University of Wisconsin–Madison's School of Library and Information Studies, Chairs Louise Robbins and later Christine Pawley provided support along with Professor Emeritus Wayne Wiegand.

Duke University's Center for Documentary Studies Summer Video Institute, Joe Lambert from the Center for Digital Storytelling–Berkeley, and the Digital StoryLab in Copenhagen, Denmark, helped me to visualize Regina's story in a different medium. Student Alexandra "Al" Ritchie from the Undergraduate Research Scholars at the University of Wisconsin–Madison edited the digital stories I created for each chapter of the book.

University of Wisconsin–Madison's librarian, Emilie Ngo-Nguidjol Songolo, negotiated access to the ProQuest Historical Black Newspapers database. Morag Walsh, Senior Archival Specialist, Special Collections and Preservation Division, Chicago Public Library provided additional assistance about Regina's early library career at her institution.

I had the opportunity to present portions of this project in a variety of settings, including Greg Downey's History of American Librarianship and Cherene Sherrard Johnson's Harlem Renaissance Women Writers classes. Nan Enstad invited me to present to the Program in Gender and Women's History. I presented internationally at the Royal School of Library and Information Science at the Black Diamond in Copenhagen and at the Collegium for African American Research (CAAR) in Paris. The Retired New York Public Librarians in New York City and Kathryn Simmons and Dr. Dianne Hopkins of the Madison African American Genealogy Writing Group invited me to speak. I was also on a panel, "Recovering Black Women Writers from the Harlem Renaissance & Beyond," at the Wisconsin Book Festival in 2012.

I enjoyed the hospitality at The Library Hotel in New York City where I stayed numerous times during the project. The book was also partially written in numerous cafes including Barriques in Fitchburg, Wis.; Lov's Bog Café, Riccos, Café Plantagen, and the Next Door Cafe in Copenhagen; and various Coffee Bean & Tea Leaf, Starbucks, and Peet's in different Los Angeles locations.

Finally, I would like to thank Regina Andrews's family. In Los Angeles in January 2009, I had the pleasure of meeting her niece, Lorelei Simms; her son, Anthony Turner, and his children; her daughters Regina Gibson-Broome and Angelina Turner and their late sister Cynthia's son and grandchild; and her cousin Pamela Anderson. I received email correspondence from Regina's grandchildren Robyn and Kim Baptiste.

Regina Anderson Andrews
Harlem Renaissance Librarian

Introduction

While reading background literature for another project, I came across an article about the role of the 135th Street Branch of the New York Public Library (NYPL) in the lives of African Americans during the Harlem Renaissance.[1] This essay mentioned that the Caucasian head librarian, the legendary Ernestine Rose, hired several African American female librarians to work at this branch.[2] I was instantly intrigued and puzzled. Who were they? Why hadn't I heard of these women? I wanted to know more about their lives.

As a female African American former Librarian-in-Residence at Yale University, I was fascinated by these African American women who entered the profession at a time when their numbers were infinitesimal. As I learned more about Regina Anderson Andrews (1901–1993), she soon emerged as one of the most interesting librarians for several reasons. She defied the stereotype of a spinster, bookish librarian. She cohosted a salon during the Harlem Renaissance and was an active participant in the little theater movement as both an actress and playwright. She had several paramours and at least one was possibly a secret—and unlike many of her contemporary white female librarians who were often single and childless, Regina married, like many of the pioneering female African American librarians, including at least four— Augusta Baker (1911–1998), Jean Blackwell Hutson (1914–1998), Alethia Annette Phinazee (1920–1983), and Dorothy Porter Wesley (1905–1995)—who married twice! Unlike schoolteachers, librarians did not have to resign their positions when they married. These women often had children too, and both Regina and Hutson adopted baby daughters. Regina had another admirer after her wedding, but whether or not the liaison was consummated is undetermined. What is known is that several years after declaring his love for her he was executed in his native Russia. During the second half of her library career she was involved in women's and African American civic organizations that led to her traveling to four continents. Finally, pictures of Regina show that she possessed movie star glamour—indeed she graced the cover of the *Messenger* in December 1924.

Generally, Regina has disappeared from the history books, save for her approximately five-year involvement with the little theater movement as an actress, playwright, and executive director, which has recently been of increasing interest to black feminist theater historians who examine her plays in dissertations, book chapters, and journal articles. Ironically, her nearly half-century groundbreaking career as a librarian is often mentioned only as an afterthought and has received scant attention by scholars in the field of library and information science.

Although Regina was interviewed for and included in key books about the Harlem Renaissance, such as Nathan Huggins's *Voices from the Harlem Renaissance* and David Levering Lewis's *When Harlem Was in Vogue*, and mentioned in Cheryl Wall's *Women of the Harlem Renaissance*, no one has written a book-length manuscript about this extraordinary woman whose life spanned almost the entire twentieth century. She lived through World Wars I and II, the Chicago Race Riots, the cold war, the Civil Rights Movement, and both the 1935 and 1964 Harlem Riots among other events. Most books about Harlem Renaissance artists and intellectuals mention the significant role of the 135th Street Branch library on their work; however, few books have been written from the perspective of the librarian.

My biography, *Harlem Renaissance Librarian*, restores her to her rightful place in history. By using a black feminist theory perspective, I will demonstrate how she negotiated her personal, creative, professional, and civic lives by refusing to be limited by traditional roles because of either her race or her gender. The central argument of my book is that Regina Andrews resisted racial stereotypes and to a lesser degree challenged expected gender roles too. I argue that her social class (upper-middle) helped to give her the strength, the connections, and the tools to defy the expected conventions of her times.

While this biography tells the story of one woman's life, it is illustrative of other New Negro women who belonged to what W. E. B. Du Bois called the Talented Tenth—the small minority of upper-class, educated African Americans whom he believed could uplift the masses out of poverty. Regina's socioeconomic background, including her parents' education and professions, her educational background, and even the geographic location of her birth is typical of other female African American librarians who were her peers. Scholar Lelia Gaston Rhodes interviewed fifteen of these women who attained success in librarianship, including pioneers Augusta Baker, Eliza Atkins Gleason, Jean Blackwell Hutson, Clara Stanton Jones, and Dorothy Porter Wesley. Rhodes found nearly half of the women had a college-educated parent including two whose parents each had a master's degree. One's father had a medical degree, although the most common occupation involved education, including many teachers and one parent who also was a college president. Generally these women came from middle-class to upper-class backgrounds. Several were born in the North, but most were southern-born. Like Regina, most of these women received their bachelor degrees at what are now known as historically black institutions. However, many attended library schools at predominantly white institutions, including the University of Michigan, University of Illinois, and Regina's alma mater, Columbia University. Only two attended library school at the African American Hampton Institute. Regina never said why she decided to become a librarian, but these women cited several reasons including a desire to serve African Americans, to uplift the race, and the prestige of the position—sentiments echoed in Elise McDougald's essay, "The Task of Negro Womanhood," originally published in Alain Locke's anthology the *New Negro*. McDougald, the first African American principal in New York City, suggested that librarianship was an ideal, respectable career for middle-class African American women:

> Comparatively new are opportunities in the field of trained library work for the Negro woman. In New York City, the Public Library system has opened its service to the employment of colored women of college grade. The vision of those in charge of their training is illuminated by fires that have somewhat of a missionary glow. There is an ever-present hope that once trained, the Negro woman librarian will scatter such opportunities across the country, establishing branches wherever none exist. . . . [S]everal others have been assigned to branches throughout the city where there is little or no Negro patronage. They are thus rendering exceptional service, and additionally creating an impetus for the enlargement of this field for Negro women.[3]

Sadly, the women that Rhodes interviewed shared another thing in common with Regina—roadblocks were placed in their paths as librarians but they were able to overcome these obstacles.[4]

When Regina applied for a job at NYPL, librarianship had not been recognized as a profession for very long. The beginning of the American Library Association (ALA) is traced to a meeting of ninety men and thirteen women in Philadelphia in 1876. Few African Americans were employed in the field when Regina joined the profession. By 1920, there were 15,297 librarians according to the Census. However, only 47 African American women and 22 African American men listed librarian as their occupation, which equaled less than half of 1 percent.[5]

Although Regina was just one of several African American women librarians who are considered important leaders in the field, it was notably African American men who were among the earliest librarians. Edward Christopher Williams (1871–1929) was the first professionally trained African American librarian. He took a leave of absence from his job as the university librarian at Western Reserve where he taught library courses to attend the New York State Library School in Albany. He received his degree in 1900.[6] Williams received a Julius Rosenwald Fellowship in 1929 to pursue a doctoral degree in library science at Columbia University. However, he became ill and died before he was able to complete the program. Other early African American librarians included bibliographer Daniel Alexander Payne Murray (1811–1893), who began working at the Library of Congress in 1871, and Richard Greener (1824–1922), the university librarian at the University of South Carolina in 1875.[7] Greener was also the first African American graduate of Harvard (Class of 1870) and ironically the estranged father of librarian Belle da Costa Greene (1883–1950), who began working at Princeton University in 1902 before she helped to establish the Morgan Library by working for financier and art collector John Pierpont (J. P.) Morgan from 1905 until her retirement in 1948. Although Greene was among the earliest African American women to enter the profession, she is not frequently mentioned as a pioneering librarian because she passed for white throughout her career.[8]

Regina developed her own racial identity and conception of what it meant to be American through details of her childhood and young adulthood as a child of mixed-race parents. Her mother, Margaret Simons (1876–?), was an artist and black clubwoman from the Midwest. Her New Orleans–born father was a well-known and controversial defense attorney, William G. "Habeas Corpus" Anderson (1870–1950), whose clients included pugilist Jack Johnson, and who unsuccessfully fought with Ida B. Wells-Barnett to save the life of his client, Thomas Jennings, who was convicted in a landmark case involving the use of fingerprints. Regina later cited Wells-Barnett as an influence when she wrote an antilynching play during the Harlem Renaissance.

When Regina was ten years old, her parents divorced over allegations of her father's infidelity, and she spent several years in predominantly white Normal, Illinois, with her maternal grandparents and where future presidential candidate Adlai Stevenson was a friend and classmate. After returning to Chicago and graduating from Hyde Park High School in 1919, Regina briefly attended the historically black institution, Wilberforce University, where she worked as a library assistant at their Carnegie Library possibly under the tutelage of African American librarian Mary Effie Lee Newsome (1885–1979).[9] Andrew Carnegie's Foundation was responsible for funding several African American public and college libraries during the beginning of the twentieth century. Regina left before graduating and returned to Chicago; she was admitted into the Chicago Public Library's apprentice training program and obtained a position as a library assistant. At the beginning of the twentieth century, librarians received training through a variety of methods including attending summer school courses, enrolling in a limited number of library schools, or training in apprentice programs at major public libraries.[10] Luckily, Chicago Public Library was one of the apprentice training programs that did not prohibit or limit the number of African Americans who could enroll.

The Chicago Public Library was where Regina became acquainted with Vivian Harsh (1890–1960), who in 1924 became the first African American librarian to head her own branch. Regina later cited Harsh as a mentor. Because the Chicago Public Library used the civil service examination system to hire librarians, Regina was not subjected to the racial pigeonholing she would encounter at NYPL. During 1922, Regina took a fateful vacation to New York City—possibly to escape a tragedy at home. She decided to remain—angering the Chicago Public Library.

Regina was assigned to the 135th Street Branch library at the beginning of the Harlem Renaissance. The commencement of the Harlem Renaissance has been difficult to define and is the subject of frequent debates. Many cite the Civic Club Dinner of March 21, 1924, which Regina attended, as the beginning of the Harlem Renaissance. This was a time when educated, upper-class African American intellectuals, writers, poets, musicians, teachers, doctors, lawyers, visual artists, and social scientists converged in the New York City neighborhood of Harlem. They produced nonfiction books and essays, novels, plays, poetry, visual art, and magazines among many other works depicting a range of African American life, although the primary objective was usually to uplift the race by countering prevailing views of African Americans as lazy, shiftless, and uncouth. Known primarily as an artistic and literary movement, the Harlem Renaissance was also a sociopolitical and intellectual movement. Until recently, male members of the Harlem Renaissance were the primary focus of publications about this time period. The contributions of women have recently been recognized.[11]

Regina was one of the librarians who supported these newcomers; she "set aside a small work area for African American writers in the library, and Langston Hughes, Eric Walrond, and Claude McKay were among its users."[12] While there, she helped to organize the North Harlem Community Forum with George Schuyler as chair of the committee that invited such controversial guests as anthropologist Franz Boas and birth control advocate Margaret Sanger to speak. Through her job, Regina came in contact with many artists whom she invited to her salon in an apartment at 580 St. Nicholas Avenue in the Sugar Hill section of Harlem, where Academy Award–nominated actress/singer Ethel Waters was a neighbor. Her roommates included Ethel Ray (later Nance), Charles S. Johnson's secretary at *Opportunity*, the house organ for the National Urban League. Ethel brought many of the writers, poets, and artists published through contests the magazine sponsored into Regina's circle. Contest winner Zora Neale Hurston was invited to sleep on the couch of their home when she first arrived in New York City. One of the most famous photos of the Harlem Renaissance, featuring Charles S. Johnson, Langston Hughes, E. Franklin Frazier, Rudolph Fisher, and Hubert Delany, was taken at 580. When African American artists arrived in New York City and told cab drivers to take them to "580," the drivers knew where to go. The apartment was immortalized in Carl Van Vechten's notorious 1926 novel *Nigger Heaven*, and some speculate that Regina was the model for the novel's librarian Mary Love. Van Vechten was banned from their parties after the book was published. Aaron Douglas, Langston Hughes, Jean Toomer, Countee Cullen, Paul Robeson, Eric Walrond, and James Weldon Johnson were just some of the people who dropped by. One scholar noted that these "parties . . . have passed into legend."[13]

Through this circle of friends, Regina met her second fiancé, one of Harlem's most eligible bachelors, Howard University and Columbia Law School graduate William T. Andrews Jr. (1898–1984), known as Bill. He would become an NAACP lawyer and assemblyman. He was the son of a Sumter, South Carolina, lawyer, newspaper publisher, and acquaintance of Booker T. Washington. Regina's maid of honor was Harlem Renaissance novelist Jessie Fauset, who hosted the wedding in her home.

After her 1926 wedding, Regina became involved with W. E. B. Du Bois's KRIGWA Players theater group housed in the basement of the 135th Street Branch. Regina later helped create the Harlem Experimental Theatre (HET) and became the first executive director, an actress, and a playwright. By writing plays, Regina joined a long line of other New Negro women writers such as Angelina Weld Grimke, Georgia Douglas Johnson, May Miller, Eulalie Spence, and Marita Bonner. Scholars Lorraine Elena Roses and Ruth Elizabeth Randolph described these women, including Regina, as "highly educated." They attended both white and black institutions, as with Regina's affiliation with Wilberforce. Despite their education, the authors noted that these women often faced racial discrimination at their places of employment—an experience Regina shared. She differed from most of these women because a large number of the African American women playwrights did not marry. Relatedly, many of these women writers were also childless, unlike Regina.[14] After the demise of KRIGWA Players, Regina helped establish the Harlem Experimental Theatre. Using a pseudonym, she wrote plays about lynching, passing, and the Underground Railroad and, unlike her fellow African American female playwrights, her protagonists were men. The theater company produced two of her plays, and she acted in other productions, earning good reviews for both her acting and writing from several African American newspapers, including the *New York Amsterdam News*, the *Chicago Defender*, and the *New York Age*. The end of the HET during the mid-1930s coincided with the end of the Harlem Renaissance. Historian David Levering Lewis cited several reasons for the end of this movement, including the economic toll of the Great Depression, the consequential focus of the NAACP and the Urban League on social and economic rather than creative concerns, and because many participants in the Harlem Renaissance left Harlem.[15]

Prior to this time period, Regina enrolled in Columbia University's Library School in the fall of 1926 and was among the first students to attend the second iteration of this program. She never discussed her own library school experiences, but we know about difficulties encountered by librarians who preceded and succeeded her enrollment at Columbia. In 1922, Harlem Renaissance novelist Nella Larsen Imes became the first African American to enroll in the NYPL Library School. This school would later consolidate with Columbia University to form the Columbia University School of Library Service that Regina attended. Larsen Imes worked in the Children's Room of the 135th Street Branch library, and Ernestine Rose encouraged her to apply to the NYPL Library School, but she was not naive about the resistance that Imes might face. According to Imes's biographer George Hutchinson, "Anticipating trouble, Rose apparently sent word to the school in advance. The first item on a faculty meeting agenda of January 26, 1922, headed 'Colored Students,' states: Mrs. Imes, assistant at the 135th St. Branch may apply for admission to the School. Should we accept her?"[16] The NYPL Library School was concerned "about how the other students would react to Imes's presence and about what would happen during the annual weeklong 'inspection trip' during which students would travel up and down the Eastern states between Baltimore and Boston visiting libraries. Would people object to rooming with Imes? Would restaurants and hotels bar her entry?"[17] Another Imes's biographer, Thadious Davis, suggested that Imes had been discouraged from enrolling in the program that granted a library degree.[18]

Dorothy Porter Wesley described her experiences attending library school at Columbia five years after Regina enrolled:

> I don't know how to describe it, except that there were a lot of negative things going on. . . . [T]he teacher with whom I was doing my major work told me that I couldn't get through with it; I came from "inferior background." She knew I couldn't do the work, and why did I want to stay? This was in October, the beginning of the year. . . . So it was a struggle with some of the teachers. Some of them were very nice. I believe, though, if this woman that I was doing my major work for—it was cataloging and classification, and I don't like to talk about it too much—she acted like she didn't want me to ever come too near her, you know, "Just don't come to [*sic*] near me." But she happened to break her leg in the beginning of the semester, and I think having her out, I was able to get through and graduate. So it never bothered me.[19]

During the same time period, Augusta Baker had her own battles with the library school at Albany State Teachers College. Eleanor Roosevelt, the wife of then New York state governor Franklin Delano Roosevelt, had to intervene on Baker's behalf in order for her to get fair treatment from the institution.[20] Baker would later become a storyteller specialist at the Countee Cullen Branch of the New York Public Library. In 1961, she became the first African American librarian to hold a systemwide administrative position at NYPL when she was appointed the coordinator of children's services for all the branches. Future librarian Audre Lorde (1934–1992) credited Baker for teaching her how to read.[21]

A year before Regina enrolled at Columbia, Hampton Institute (now Hampton University) established the first library school (1925–1939) at an African American college after receiving funding from the Rosenwald Fund, the Carnegie Corporation, and the General Education Board—organizations concerned about the education of African Americans. Virginia Lacy Jones (1912–1984) received her bachelor of science from Hampton in 1933 and later became a faculty member at Atlanta University library school when it was established in 1941, joining North Carolina Central, which still exists, as the second and third library school programs established at African American institutions.[22] Jones joined Atlanta University's Library School Dean Eliza Atkins Gleason (1909–2009)—the first African American to receive a doctorate in the field when she graduated in 1940 from the University of Chicago's Graduate School of Library Science. In 1945, Jones became the second African American to receive a doctorate in library science.

Although Regina never completed her degree at Columbia University, her NYPL career continued to flourish. By 1930, there were 29,613 librarians in the United States, and the number of African Americans listed on this Census had tripled to 30 men and 180 women for a total of 210 librarians, compared to the 69 from the 1920 Census. However, the percentage of African American librarians still was less than 1 percent. The increase in the number of African American librarians was likely attributable to the establishment of the library school at Hampton Institute in the intervening years.

African American librarians in the 1930s were not the only ones in a precarious position. From the beginning of the twentieth century, public library services for African Americans had a troubled history.[23] According to findings of a study conducted by white librarian Louis Shores, published in 1930, things were still in a state of flux.[24] Shores surveyed public libraries in eighty cities with the largest numbers of African Americans as determined by the U.S. Census. He asked about the types of library services offered to African American patrons, employment of African American librarians, and opportunities for enrollment in library apprentice training programs. Shores classified his results into five types of library services offered to African Americans. Many cities offered no library services for African Americans, including Charleston, South Carolina; Dallas, Texas; Jackson, Mississippi; Miami, Florida; Mobile, Alabama; Raleigh, North Carolina; and Shreveport, Louisiana. Most cited a lack of funds as the reason for not having a segregated branch or vague plans for the future.

In another category were cities, such as Fort Worth, Texas, that let African American library patrons check out books for home use but did not allow them to remain in the library to read their books. In 1939, there was a sit-in at Alexandria, Virginia's public library to protest such policies. Unfortunately, the result of the sit-in was the creation of a segregated library branch for African American patrons and not the integration of the existing library. Alexandria was not alone in this policy. Many cities provided a segregated branch for African American patrons, including Atlanta, Georgia; Durham, North Carolina; Houston, Texas; Knoxville and Memphis, Tennessee; New Orleans, Louisiana; Tulsa, Oklahoma; and Richmond, Virginia. One of the earliest segregated library branches was in Louisville, Kentucky, supervised by Thomas Fountain Blue. He managed the Western Branch Library, which opened in 1905. He is recognized for developing a four-to-six–month apprentice training program for African American librarians that combined education and practical work experience. Hampton Institute later modeled their library program after Blue's training program.[25] In 1960, thirty years after Shore's survey was published, there would be another library sit-in by the "Greenville 8." Eight young adults, including future civil rights leader Jesse Jackson, entered the Greenville County Library in South Carolina and protested the segregated policies by refusing to leave. They were arrested, and after temporarily closing to thwart legal action, the library eventually reopened as an integrated one.

Some cities had a "Negro" branch placed in communities with large numbers of African Americans. However, these were not segregated branches, because African Americans were not restricted to using only that particular branch but had access to all other branches in the cities. This was the case in Chicago when "two colored assistants"—most likely Regina and Vivian Harsh—were described as working at the Abraham Lincoln Center Branch in the early 1920s in a report about African American public library services.[26] Many of the "Negro" branches employed African American library assistants to provide services and programs. These cities included Baltimore, Maryland; Chicago, Illinois; Cincinnati, Ohio; Detroit, Michigan; Los Angeles, California; New York, New York; and Bartlesville, Oklahoma, where an unidentified librarian speculated that African Americans, especially children, would read more if there were more books "about their life." This librarian was no doubt white librarian Ruth Brown, who ran Bartlesville Public Library for thirty years until her unceremonious dismissal in 1950. Ostensibly she was fired for having subversive material in her collection, but scholar Louise S. Robbins cogently argued that Brown's involvement with civil rights advocate Bayard Rustin and the Congress of Racial Equality (CORE) and her integration of children's story time were among the real reasons for her dismissal.[27] The final category included cities that granted full access to all library branches to African American patrons, including Boston, Massachusetts, and Cleveland, Ohio.

Back in New York City, in 1937, the African American newspaper the *Amsterdam News* reported that several African American civic leaders, including the head of the New York Urban League and several attorneys, queried Franklyn Hopper, the NYPL chief of the circulation department and responsible for hiring librarians, about the difficulty that African Americans had obtaining even job applications for positions in the system. The leaders also wanted to know why African Americans were told to see Ernestine Rose at the 135th Street Branch. Hopper replied, "I assume that any young Negro woman is interested in the development of work of her own people." He then made a comparison with how a young Czech applicant would be sent to the Webster Branch. He concluded by stating, "Miss Rose is, as of course you know, better qualified than anybody else in the system to introduce a young woman to the field of work with the Negroes."[28] The leaders, like the African American librarians, resisted their placement at only the "Negro" branches of the NYPL.

It was in this atmosphere that Regina broke the color barrier in 1938 by becoming the first African American Supervising Librarian in NYPL history. Her accomplishment was not an easy one. Regina fought, with W. E. B. Du Bois representing the NAACP as a powerful ally, against the NYPL administration for opportunities for promotion and equal pay. Du Bois was appalled that these librarians were restricted to working in a select few neighborhoods, noting that Chicago had fewer African Americans citizens but more African American librarians.

Regina's victory came just two years after arguably the American Library Association's most controversial annual conference. The organization decided to hold its meeting in Richmond, Virginia, which subjected African American librarians to segregated conditions. The ALA informed the African American librarians that the conference hotel would allow them to use the same entrance as the white delegates. However, "This does not mean that Negro delegates may obtain rooms and meals at these hotels as this is forbidden by Virginia law," the ALA continued. "Those meetings which are part of breakfasts, luncheons or dinners are not open to Negroes. . . . Provisions will be made to seat Negroes in the front right hand section of the main floor of the auditorium during the general sessions."[29] The American Library Association was widely condemned by its members, both African American and white, and they urged the organization to not hold their annual conferences in segregated cities in the future.

Although some African American librarians formed their own associations in their respective states because they were prohibited from joining their state's library association, surprisingly, there would not be a national professional association for African American librarians until several decades later when the Black Caucus of the American Library Association (BCALA) was established at the midwinter meeting of the ALA in 1970. According to the mission and purpose of the BCALA, it serves "as an advocate for the development, promotion, and improvement of library services and resources to the nation's African American community; and provides leadership for the recruitment and professional development of African American librarians."[30]

The first African American librarian would not be elected to the presidency of the ALA until a few years later in 1976, when Clara Stanton Jones (1913–2012), the director of the Detroit Public Library, was voted into office.[31] Jones was later followed by E. J. Josey (1924–2009) in 1983 as the first African American male elected president of ALA.

While battling the NYPL, Regina and her husband, Bill—then an assemblyman representing Harlem—expanded their family by adopting a mixed-race daughter, Regina Ann. She tried to balance work with raising a child. Letters suggested that the relationship between mother and daughter was not an easy one, which ironically recalled Regina's relationship with her own mother. As if she was not busy enough with work and family, she became active in civic organizations.

Regina served as the vice president of the National Council of Women of the United States—an interracial women's organization cofounded by Susan B. Anthony. In 1953, when she joined this organization, there was a lack of a strong black feminist movement, which may account for why, unlike her mother, she joined this interracial organization that had a history of being more accepting of African Americans than other organizations. No doubt Regina was also influenced by her mother's own involvement as a black club-woman in the Necessity Club in Chicago at the beginning of the twentieth century.

Regina was also on the board of trustees for twenty-two years for the Urban League of New York. She represented both organizations as a United Nations (UN) observer and as a commission member with the United Nations Educational, Scientific and Cultural Organization (UNESCO). One of her main professional interests involved facilitating understanding among various immigrant groups. Through her work as a UN observer, Regina became an acquaintance of ambassadors from around the world, whom she invited to speak at her library's program, Family Night at the Library. This program was modeled on her earlier work at the 115th Street Branch, where invited guests included Eleanor Roosevelt, an acquaintance of both Regina and her father. Her gender, race, and social class status made her an ideal and noncontentious representative of U.S. racial politics. More outspoken African Americans such as W. E. B. Du Bois and Paul Robeson had their international travel curtailed because the State Department revoked their passports. Regina had an opportunity to travel to several continents. Only NYPL's mandatory retirement policy ended Regina's long career.

The Andrews spent their retirement in Mahopac, New York, where they owned a 1799 New England–style home in Putnam County—their weekend retreat since the early 1940s. Regina was actively involved in the Mahopac community and invited singer Marian Anderson (no relation) to an event she hosted. Her retirement was not entirely tranquil. Regina was a member of a three-person panel that included historian John Henrik Clarke to consult on the 1969 *Harlem on My Mind* exhibition that opened with protests outside of the Metropolitan Museum of Art. One scholar called the resulting exhibit "one of the most controversial exhibitions ever mounted by an American museum."[32] One positive outcome of the exhibit was the posthumous publication of *The Black New Yorkers* from an unused manuscript that Regina created for the exhibit. Her beloved Bill died in 1984 after fifty-eight years of marriage. She outlived him by nearly a decade, leaving a powerful legacy.

Nearly one hundred years after Regina Anderson Andrews began her library career, there are currently 216,000 librarians in the United States and a little over 9 percent are African American.[33] There are no longer racial barriers to enrollment in library schools, and the most recent statistics for the number of African Americans graduating with a master's degree in library and information science and enrolled in library school indicated that during the 2010–2011 academic year 54 African American men and 278 African American women received master's degrees, for a total of 332, or a little over 4 percent of all students obtaining degrees. In the fall 2011 semester, there were 123 African American males and 664 African American females enrolled in master's of library and information science programs, for a total of 787 students, or close to 4 percent of total student enrollment.[34]

Regina was among the small number of first-generation African American female librarians who forged a career in a sometimes unwelcoming profession that did not always embrace their attempts to obtain an education through library schools or apprentice training programs and employment opportunities outside of segregated or "colored" library branches. This biography increases our understanding of the personal and professional lives of these women and the strategies employed to counter the obstacles they faced.

Chapter 1 begins with Regina's job interview at the NYPL and describes Regina's early childhood and her parents' background information. Chapter 2 details Regina's years in Normal, Illinois, and then shifts to her return to Chicago and her college experiences at Wilberforce University. In Chapter 3, Regina becomes part of the Harlem Renaissance upon her arrival in New York City. Chapter 4 chronicles her romances and culminates in her marriage. Regina's involvement with the Harlem Experimental Theatre is the subject of Chapter 5, and her decades-long battle with the NYPL is captured in Chapter 6. The focus of Chapter 7 is Regina's involvement with civic organizations, including associated international travels. Chapter 8 describes Regina's active retirement years and discusses her legacy.

1. Chicago

The Beginning

In 1923, when Regina, as a librarian, decided to remain in New York City, it seemed like the most obvious thing to do would be to seek employment at the largest library system in the city—the New York Public Library. Although Regina lived with family in Chicago and had a good job at the Chicago Public Library, she decided she wanted something different, or perhaps she was escaping from a tragedy back home. Regina was also finding "it difficult to fit into the comfortable and complacent middle-class society that was expected of Negro young ladies."[1]

Three or four days after she completed the application at the main branch, she received a request to return for an interview. One could imagine that Regina was probably very nervous as she entered the 42nd Street Branch library on Fifth Avenue, an imposing beaux arts building designed by architects John Merven Carrere and Thomas Hastings. The edifice had existed only for a little over a decade, opening May 24, 1911, when Regina arrived for her appointment. No doubt she was impeccably clad, as usual, and her waist-length hair was most likely pinned up since Regina "combed it very high on her head in a Spanish fashion."[2] In fact, she possessed long hair for her entire life. Although the current style was bobbed hair, Regina's father paid her to keep it long. She entered the building by passing through the two gigantic lion statues, nicknamed either Leo Astor and Leo Lenox or Lady Astor and Lord Lenox at that time. They are now known as Patience and Fortitude, after being renamed by then mayor Fiorello La Guardia during the Depression to reflect the characteristics that he suggested New Yorkers needed during this difficult time.

Regina had been described as "a beautiful, beautiful girl"[3] and "a pert olive-skinned girl."[4] In fact, the next year, in December 1924, she graced the cover of the *Messenger: World's Greatest Negro Monthly*. At the beginning of that year, the magazine declared that it would "show in pictures as well as writing, Negro women who are unique, accomplished, beautiful, intelligent, industrious, talented and successful."[5] Regina fit that description. On the cover she posed in a three-quarter profile and looked very elegant with her hair loosely styled in a nonlibrarianlike bun with curly bangs covering her forehead.

Instead of focusing on her previous library experience at Chicago's Hyde Park High School, Wilberforce University, and the Chicago Public Library, the personnel administrator was most concerned about her race. He asked her, "What do you mean where you have here under race and religion you have American?"

Regina replied, "Well, I always considered myself an American. I don't know what else I could be."

He asked her, "What is your background?"

Like untold numbers of U.S. citizens, Regina came from a multicultural background requiring a roadmap to follow. Her father, William Grant Anderson, a prominent criminal defense attorney in Chicago, sprang from the union of a Swedish immigrant and his American Indian wife. Regina's maternal grandfather, Reverend Henry Simons, was the son of an Arkansas Confederate General and an immigrant Jewish woman. Henry's wife, Regina's maternal grandmother Lucinda Reynolds, was the offspring of a Madagascar mother and an East Indian father.[6] Regina considered herself an American. She explained her complicated history to her interlocutor.

He replied, "To us you're not an American. You're not white."[7]

*　＊　＊*

The day in Chicago was "cool and generally fair."[8] In the Hyde Park section, rain patted the roof of 4609 Vincennes Avenue, a two-story house rented by a lawyer and his artist wife. William and Margaret Anderson lived with their three-year-old son, Maurice Barton; one-year-old daughter, Mildred Viola (assuming she was still alive); Margaret's younger sister, Kathryn Simons, a stenographer; her older brother, Eugene Simons, a porter for the railroad; and a servant, Mary Watson. Under the category of "race," the entire household was designated as black. The majority of the neighbors were white immigrants from England and Germany, although the Andersons were not the only black residents. The neighborhood had two physicians, a shoe store clerk, a musician, clerks, a stenographer, a clothing salesman, a mercantile office worker, and servants. From the time of her birth into the Anderson household on Tuesday, May 21, 1901, Regina Mathilde Anderson would come to view herself in nonracialized terms.

Regina described her maternal grandfather as "[t]all with a splendid physique, with long white hair and beautiful blue eyes." Margaret's father, Henry Simons, was listed as mulatto on the 1870 Census, black on the 1910 Census, and white on the 1920 Census. Her mother, Lucinda, was also described as mulatto. Their daughter Margaret Helen Simons arrived in 1876, the sixth of seven children. Margaret would be listed as a mulatto on Regina's revised birth certificate. Racial designations for both sides of Regina's family would continue to be confusing and represent the difficulty that the U.S. Census recorders had in designating race.

Regina once described her mother as a, "well known china painter—World's Fair."[9] As a teenager Margaret exhibited her work at the Columbian Exhibition in 1893.[10] Regina later recalled that her mother was "a beautiful artist."[11] In a 1980 letter, Alfreda Duster, Ida B. Wells-Barnett's daughter, informed Regina that, "I have the beautiful china set your mother painted by hand for my mother's wedding. As I heard it—she painted the sugar bowl, creamer, teapot and a few place settings commissioned by the Ida B. Wells Woman's Club, and each year another place setting until the set had at least 6 place settings. There may have been more than that, because when I was in California a few years ago, my Aunt Lil had one of the dinner plates."[12] Pictures of Margaret as an adult show her as a stout, full-figured, big-boned woman who possessed her father's full cheeks, in contrast to her sister Kathreen, two years her junior, who was sharp-featured. Variously called Katherine, Kathreen, Kathryn, or Kate, she would often live with and figure prominently in the life of her niece Regina. Margaret would raise two children into adulthood and would suffer the tragic loss of two daughters.

*　*　*

Regina's father William Grant Anderson was only a few days old when an enumerator for the 1870 Census visited his household. He was born on April 27, 1870, in New Orleans, Louisiana. He was designated a mulatto on the 1870 Census with the rest of his family and later listed as Brown on Regina's revised birth certificate. William's father, Alexander, owned a barbershop, and his wife Sarah's occupation was listed as "keeping house." Family lore hinted that Regina's grandfather was a Swedish immigrant—but evidence suggested that he was born in Louisiana. Perhaps an earlier relative was born in Sweden, which accounts for a derivation of their last name. William was Alexander and Sarah's seventh child.

In 1880 several family members were living in St. Louis, Missouri. Sarah was now a widow and thirty-seven years old—somehow seemed even younger than she was a decade earlier. Lacking literacy skills and as the new head of the household, Sarah supported the four children who still lived with her by "renting furnished rooms."[13] William, listed as "Willy," was ten and had three sisters, ages thirteen, nine, and four. Eventually, Sarah, William, and a few siblings made their way to Chicago, either in 1880 or 1882. Regina described her grandmother:

> I have a faint memory of the Indian Grandmother who had left New Orleans with her small son and two baby daughters to seek a new home, first in Missouri and then in Illinois. I can remember my great awe and curiosity over this Grandmother's long silences as she spent her last years in a hard backed chair, by the fire. Seldom speaking or sharing in the new life of her grown son and his family, she lived to see them securely settled in the Hyde Park area of Chicago. She too, was there, but some part of her had long ago returned to the land of her Fathers.

William, as the oldest child and the only son in the house, probably felt responsible for helping his mother to support the family.[14] He was very young to be doing the types of jobs that he did. Regina recalled visiting her father in Chicago around 1942 to watch him "win a terrific case." After court, Regina's father showed her his name inscribed, "on an old stone hitching post dedicated to the newspaper boys who delivered their papers despite the famous blizzard."[15] He also worked as an office boy before leaving to attend school. William "was regarded as an exceptionally bright scholar and was the recognized leader of his class."[16] Eventually, he was able to study shorthand at the West Chicago Evening School and mastered this skill in three months. He sought a job at a law office as a stenographer and clerk when he was just fifteen years old. At twenty-one he was appointed as the official stenographer for the Probate Clerk's Office, "one of the highest political honors which has ever been bestowed upon the Colored race in the State of Illinois, and coming from the Democrats, the event is all the more important."[17] William was awarded this position by undertaking "a competitive exam . . . resulting in his favor."[18] His future offspring, Regina, would also gain a position by taking an examination and did not have to deal with the vagaries of racism to obtain a job in Chicago.

William made his first political speech during the 1888 26th Presidential election when Republican Benjamin Harrison was elected over Democrat Grover Cleveland. William was called "a champion of the Colored man's rights, and argued upon the broad theory that a division of votes of Afro-Americans between the Republican and Democratic parties would result in an effort being made to secure them by both parties." The reporter suggested "his past career to other young men for emulation."[19] A stenographer by day,

William worked toward his law degree at night. He was admitted to the bar in 1896—the year he married.

There was no doubt that William was quite a catch. A sketch of William shows a handsome young man sporting a mustache probably worn to make him look more mature. He appeared to be light-skinned with receding semi-curly hair. He was a self-made man rising from a working-class family. He might not have been attractive to African American women who came from a long line of middle-class or upper-class college-educated people because he lacked a strong pedigree as the son of a barber and an illiterate mother. Nevertheless, his salary was impressive and his ambition was to be admired. Margaret was also considered quite a catch according to their wedding announcement, which called her "accomplished" and "a most popular and worthy young woman, well known throughout the state."[20]

Regina's parents wed on Friday, June 12, 1896; William was twenty-six years old, and Margaret was twenty. The wedding and reception lasted nearly the entire day and spanned two states. Six hundred invitations went out for the wedding and the reception, and they were married in Margaret's father's church in Marion, Indiana, at 10 o'clock in the morning; her father, Reverend Henry Simons, officiated. The wedding was predicted to be "the event of the season." Attorney Fred W. Burrows served as William's best man. The article did not mention who served as Margaret's maid or matron of honor—most likely one of her sisters. After the wedding, the couple, family, and members of the wedding party hopped on the 12 o'clock train for the one hundred and fifty-mile ride to Chicago scheduled to arrive at five P.M. The wedding reception lasted from seven to ten that same evening and was held in William's home on 3449 Dearborn Street. The next day the "happy couple" was off on a nearly two-week honeymoon visiting various midwestern towns, including "Waukesha, St. Paul, Minneapolis and Lake Minnetonka." They would return to Chicago around June 23rd and presumably lived in William's home for a few years before moving to 4609 Vincennes Avenue, where they resided when Regina was born in 1901.

The family lived in that house from 1900 to 1902 before buying an 1889 single-family home nearby at 530 East Forty-Fifth Street.[21] The new neighborhood consisted of mainly white residents. The Andersons were the only people of color on their block, and they were now listed as *mulattoes*. Their neighbors' occupations consisted of grocer proprietor, another lawyer, clerks, sales lady, servants, salesman, engineer, and a physician. By 1910, the household consisted of both parents, twelve-year-old Maurice, nine-year-old Regina, a new sister, Mercedes Alice, who was five, and Aunt Kathreen, who now worked as a teacher. Sister Mildred Viola appears to have died, since she is no longer listed on the Census. Although the household now had three children, there was no longer a servant to help Margaret, whose occupation was listed as "artist," and William, who continued his work as an attorney.

Regina described her memories of growing up in Chicago: "I remember the deep winter snows soon grimy with coal dust and the far flung odors of the stock yards in sultry summers. The heat of the dry summer days was cooled by Lake Michigan." She recalled nearby Jackson Park "with its rapidly deteriorating World's Fair Building." She continued, "There was Washington Park where my brother and I rode our ponies along the bridal path to the Midway."[22]

*   *   *

No doubt Regina learned about fighting an unjust system where race was concerned through her father's work as a defense attorney. His legal exploits were reported in both the African American and white press—the *Chicago Defender* and the *Chicago Daily Tribune*, respectively. As an attorney, Anderson defended noble causes like civil rights violations and saved many innocent African Americans from wrongful jail sentences. In at least one case, the *Green* case, he saved a man from an inevitable lynching. Regina recalled that she "was quite at home in the court with him" and that she "used to go down to Joliet prison" when he was meeting with his clients. She remembered that her father was "very happy when he won cases and we would go out to celebrate."[23] His use of the writ of habeas corpus was so widespread and successful that he earned the nickname, William G. "Habeas Corpus" Anderson.

Some of Anderson's legal work was more profitable than noble. However, he often worked on more virtuous causes in partnership with E. (Edward) H. Wright, destined to become the leader of his time in black politics.[24] Anderson also worked with attorney Ferdinand Barnett, the husband of noted antilynching advocate and journalist Ida B. Wells-Barnett.[25] He was acquainted with Wells-Barnett because they often united in fighting for the freedom of African American men. Regina was nine when the events surrounding the *Green* case took place. She probably heard her father discussing the case, and may have met Wells-Barnett in her home. On August 20, 1910, the *Chicago Daily Tribune* reported that Steve Green confessed to killing a white plantation agent "[a]fter having protested his innocence . . . for five days."[26] Green would be returned to Arkansas where he would no doubt face a lynch mob for killing a white man.

A week later, the *Chicago Defender* reported that, "Monday night while the storm was raving and rain and lightning seemed to rent the very earth,"

Green was rescued from the Arkansas sheriff in Cairo, Illinois, at the train station a few miles away from the state line. The African American newspaper reported that Green wanted to seek employment elsewhere because he was not being paid. His employer refused to let him go. A scuffle ensued. As his attorney, Anderson told the press:

> Green's fear that he will be thrown into a bonfire is not without foundation.
> . . . He insists that he killed the planter, William Sadler, in self-defense, but if
> he had the best defense in the world it would not avail him in Arkansas. The
> many lynchings there prove it. The fact that the prisoner was turned over to
> the custody of a sheriff does not mean that he would not be lynched. The only
> guarantee that Green has that he would not be lynched when he reaches Ar-
> kansas is for the governor of the state to give the prisoner military protection.[27]

Several weeks later Green was a free man.[28] An editorial praised the work of Green's attorneys for "their bold effort and successful achievement."[29]

During the Harlem Renaissance, Regina would cite Ida B. Wells-Barnett as a childhood influence on an antilynching play that she wrote. Together with Wells-Barnett, her father also unsuccessfully fought for Thomas Jennings, an African American accused of a crime spree in September 1910 that culminated in the murder of Clarence Hiller. The alleged killer left fingerprint impressions in wet paint on a porch railing. It was "the first murder case on record in which the finger print system of identification was relied upon for a conviction."[30] One jury member said "that Anderson put the rope around his client's neck" when he questioned the ability of the fingerprint expert to make an imprint of his own fingers and the expert was able to do just that.[31] Antilynching advocate Wells-Barnett sought clemency for Jennings. She argued, "It is a well-known fact that when a crime is committed the police if possible fasten the crime upon a negro." Governor Charles S. Deneen and the state board of pardons did not commute Jennings's sentence, and he was executed.[32]

There is no evidence that Regina ever used legal means to fight perceived discrimination against the New York Public Library. However, she would gather powerful allies to champion her causes. No doubt her confidence in her ability to fight for her rights was instilled by the lessons she learned from her father. Her confidence would be sorely tested in the decades to come.

2. Normal, Illinois; Chicago; Wilberforce; and Chicago Public Library

In 1911, after sixteen years of marriage, Regina's parents divorced over allegations of infidelity against William. Margaret accused William of becoming intimate with a former client who obtained a divorce using William as her attorney. According to the *Broad Axe* newspaper, "this particular Colored lady is exceedingly good looking, and . . . most any married woman would feel a little bit uncomfortable if she would happen to get a little too close to her husband." Margaret was awarded the family home worth about $8,000 and received $90 a month for child support.[1] Apparently William was reluctant to divorce and said he tried to be a good husband and father but that no one was perfect. He cited one example to prove he was a good father. In 1909, he paid $500 to send Regina to the South because of her health.[2]

Regina was eleven at the time of the divorce and was once again sent away. This time she lived with her maternal grandfather, Rev. Henry Simons, and his second wife Laura in Normal, Illinois. Normal, a two-hour drive south from Chicago, was an ironic name for the little town because Regina's life was nowhere near normal when she arrived there to live for four years. We also do not know why the divorce sent Regina to Normal.[3] As far as can be established, both parents remained in Chicago—Margaret in the family home at 530 E. 45th Street and William most likely in the magnificent mahogany home he purchased with his legal fees. It is also not clear whether either sibling went with Regina. Apparently, seven-year-old Mercedes took her parents' divorce very hard, and maybe she was allowed to remain in Chicago—most likely with her mother.

We know little about Regina's day-to-day childhood in Chicago, but two personal letters reveal a bit about what life was like in Normal. While visiting

Normal as an adult, Regina wrote these letters to a friend, Joseph Freeman, back home in New York City. The Ukrainian-born Freeman was an editor and reporter for left-wing communist publications. He traveled and worked in various U. S. cities and abroad before returning to New York City shortly before Regina arrived. During the 1920s, he handled public relations for the American Civil Liberties Union (ACLU) and wrote about the textile workers' strike in Passaic, New Jersey. The Communist Party later denounced him after the publication of his autobiography, *An American Testament*, in 1936.[4] It is unknown how the two met, but her letters suggest more than a passing interest in Freeman beyond his potential role as a lecturer for the North Harlem Community Forum at the 135th Street Branch library.

Regina described Normal, Illinois, the location of the Illinois State University, as being very different from "Forty-Second Street and Fifth Avenue" back in New York City. She said Normal was "a quiet college town." Normal was a "veritable 'Main Street,' with its village gossips, and neighborly inquisitiveness."

Reverend Henry Simons built the home at 405 North Fell Avenue during the 1860s or 1870s. The ten-room residence sat on a quarter-block of land surrounded by "huge elms and maples." Like her mother before her, as a child Regina sat in a swing hanging from a pear tree. She slept in a "four-poster feather bed" and played with dolls and sleds except for on Sundays when the dolls were locked away. Her Sunday "occupation was sitting on the front porch reading the Bible, a stiffly starched and beribboned little girl." She used to attend Sunday school across the street at an "ivy grown church" wearing a "stiff starched little white dress" with her bible at hand.

Regina recalled:

> And today such a funny (to me) thing happened. I had gone down town [*sic*] to the hardware store to buy a paring knife for Mother. I picked out the one I wanted conscious of a peculiar silence from the other side of the counter, looked up to have it wrapped, and who should it be—the idol of our freshman football team, I dropped the knife, he laughed and so did I, when we shook hands. He said, "you are Regina, you sat in front of me and I used to pull your curls." And I—"Yes, and I spilled ink in the cuff of your new shirts and you gave me a ticket to the football game and asked me not to tell my Grandmother." And how much we had to talk about, our high school days, and all that happened since—sixteen years since I was a high school girl with black curls and his were gold. We knew nothing of race and prejudice . . . those lessons have followed.

Her experiences in Normal no doubt also contributed to how Regina came to view herself in nonracialized terms. She only reported fond memories about

Normal, Illinois. Although her family was one of few African Americans in town, she did not recall any racial incidents, as noted in her previous anecdote.

It was here in Normal that she attended school with the future Illinois governor and presidential candidate Adlai Stevenson II. Regina's grandfather "had been an early friend of Stevenson's Grandfather 'Fell.'"[5] Fell was Adlai E. Stevenson, Grover Cleveland's former vice president of the United States. Decades later Regina was an ardent supporter of Stevenson's second unsuccessful attempt to run for president. His first unsuccessful attempt was in 1952; Stevenson lost both times to Dwight D. Eisenhower. In 1956, Regina and her future husband attended a $100-per-person event at the Waldorf Astoria Grand Ballroom, and Regina also hosted a reception for Stevenson, which he attended, at her home at 409 Edgecombe Avenue—the penthouse apartment with a terrace. But, most significantly, in terms of her experiences in Normal, Regina later credited a "patient understanding librarian in the grammar school in Normal, Ill., as guiding influences in the early life and training which has done much to bring ultimate success in [my] chosen field."[6]

This home in Normal, a source of comfort and pride to Regina, would later become a source of great distress.

*   *   *

Back home in Chicago, Regina's mother, now divorced, began to pursue her interest in both art and volunteer work in earnest. Margaret variously sold her work and was employed as an instructor. It is unknown where she received her artistic training or whether she was self-taught because of limited opportunities for African Americans interested in art at that time. She took as many opportunities as were available to both display her art and to provide instruction. Margaret was an instructor at the Enterprise Institute led by President Rev. G. H. McDaniel. The other eight instructors taught more practical classes in vehicle construction and carriage trimming, dressmaking, hairdressing, manicuring, scalp treatment, barbering, plumbing, locksmithing, and gunsmithing, among many other trades. The institute was variously located at 3705 and 3711 State Street and 15 West 37th Street. McDaniel said, "It was our pleasure to meet Mrs. Margaret Anderson, instructor in China painting. Mrs. Anderson is one of the most gifted and successful instructors in this fine art in the United States."[7]

In time for the 1913 Christmas holidays, Margaret's "shop" had moved from her previous location in a room at 3518 State Street to another room. She would be "pleased to see her many patrons and those who would like to get wedding and other China articles for Christmas." A phone number was included. We do not know how successful her business was. It seems unlikely that many African American people would need china or find china painting to be a lucrative and practical career compared to other courses offered at the institute.[8]

Margaret also displayed her work at various locations in Chicago. A journalist wrote, "One of the most interesting exhibits at the Lincoln Jubilee . . . was that of china painting. . . . Mrs. Margaret H. Anderson was awarded the Blue Ribbon, her originality in design, taste and harmony of color stamps her as the greatest artist in her line among our people."[9] Regina's mother most likely influenced and encouraged her later pursuits of the arts.

Besides her interest in art, Margaret was also a clubwoman. Many affluent African American women created and joined civic organizations designed to help less fortunate African Americans. Regina, like her mother, would later volunteer by joining a national interracial women's organization, and her interest in women's issues would be more racially inclusive domestically and internationally. In 1900, the various clubs, including many in Chicago, formed the Illinois Federation of Colored Women's Clubs (IFCWC), and Regina's mother was the recording secretary for this organization.[10] Historian Anne Meis Knupfer described Chicago's Phyllis Wheatley Club and Home, which offers insight into other club's activities. The Wheatley Club "not only provided community services and camaraderie, but also served as a marker of social class, status, and prestige" and "members led lives which were far different from the recipients of their charitable deeds." Club activities included "poetry readings, dramatic renditions, and musical performances."[11] The Wheatley Club also held forums where social reform issues were discussed. Knupfer stated that most clubwomen were "college-educated, of middle-class status, and subscribed to the ideology of domestic feminism."[12] Further, "an examination of other club members' background reveals that many were either professional women or were married to prominent men in the community" like Margaret had been.[13]

In 1916, Margaret hosted the first meeting of the Necessity Club in her home. Mary Waring, who later became the president of the National Association of Colored Women (NACW), was the president, and Lena Perry, a truant officer, was the secretary of the organization. Perry also worked at the Wendell Phillips Settlement where Margaret exhibited her work in 1911.[14]

Meanwhile, after living for four years in Normal, Illinois, Regina returned to live in Chicago with her mother and sister Mercedes and to complete high school. Regina graduated from Hyde Park High School in 1919. The current incarnation, opened in 1914, is the one that Regina attended. This majestic building is located at 6220 S. Stony Island Avenue in the Woodlawn neighborhood. The building covers nearly the entire block and overlooks a park across the street. One of its most famous graduates was pilot Amelia Earhart, who graduated several months before Regina entered Hyde Park High School in the fall of 1915. An Earhart biographer, Susan Butler, said, "Hyde Park was the best public school in Chicago. Located near the University of Chicago, challenged by the infusion of the bright, motivated children of University of Chicago faculty, Hyde Park excelled in all disciplines and offered extensive extracurricular activities. Its student body was notable for the high percentage who went on to attend top colleges" and for the distinguished alumni who excelled in various fields.[15]

In the 1918 yearbook, *Aitchpe*, Regina is listed as Regina Mildred Anderson. Perhaps she assumed the middle name Mildred to honor her deceased sister. Regina was a member of the Garden Club, which held field trips and lectures, and the Girl's Athletic Association. A caption about Regina noted that, "She has been a fine student, as we all know. We seldom hear her speak, for she believes in the old adage 'Silence is Golden.'" In the 1916 edition, Regina is listed under sophomores, and next to each student's name is a quote selected by the student. Regina chose an intriguing quote: "And if she won't, she won't."[16] The full poem is:

> Where is the man who has the power and skill,
> To stem the torrent of a woman's will?
> For if she will, she will, you may depend on't;
> And if she won't, she won't; so there's an end on't.

The poem appears to be about a woman who does what she wants.

Although her high-school transcript has not been located, admissions to the College of Liberal Arts at Wilberforce, the institution Regina attended, required the completion of the following units in high school: English, Foreign Languages, Mathematics, Science, and History. Five more units must come from the following subjects: Anabasis (books), Latin, French, German, Chemistry, Physical Geography, Physics, Zoology, General Biology, History, Civics, Physiology, Botany, or Geology. No record exists of what foreign language Regina studied.

In the yearbook, next to students' captions are the names of various universities, perhaps indicative of where the student intended to attend college. Next to Regina's caption is Northwestern in nearby Evanston, Illinois. Instead, she enrolled in an entirely different university in Ohio.

Regina must have experienced culture shock when she moved from a sophisticated, urban city—Chicago—to a provincial small town to attend Wilberforce University in Xenia, Ohio, the institution named after the British abolitionist William Wilberforce. It was the oldest African American college and the first institution in the United States to have an African American president.[17]

Regina was one of forty-one women enrolled at Wilberforce University during the 1919–1920 academic year. Students came "from every part of the United States, Canada, South America, Africa, the Bermuda Islands, the Bahamas Islands and the West Indies." Many of the students came from small towns in the United States in Kentucky, Arkansas, Iowa, and Ohio, although there were a few from bigger cities represented, such as St. Louis and Kansas City, Missouri, and Cleveland, Ohio.[18]

Regina attended Wilberforce under the presidency of William Scarborough, who was born a slave. Later, both white and free black neighbors educated Scarborough, although it was illegal for a slave to read and write. In 1871 he enrolled in Oberlin College. The founder of Wilberforce, Daniel Payne, hired Scarborough to chair the Greek and Latin department in 1877. Scarborough became the vice president of the university in 1897 and was later elected president from 1908 until 1920—the end of Regina's first year at Wilberforce.[19]

During his presidency Scarborough obtained generous contributions, revised the curriculum, and increased the number of teaching faculty twofold; student enrollment increased from 400 hundred to 1,542. He was able to greatly decrease the debt and increase the endowment.

The university benefited from various financial gifts, including a generous gift from Andrew Carnegie that directly benefited Regina—money to fund the library at Wilberforce.[20] Regina worked there as an assistant librarian.[21] The Carnegie library opened on September 1, 1907, contained 10,500 bound volumes, and operated six days a week. Students studied in one of several spacious reading rooms equipped with modern furnishings.[22]

Regina enrolled in the College of Liberal Arts on the Scientific track, and tuition was $15.00 a term. Rent was $6.00 per term, fuel and light were $3, a key deposit was $2.50, and the library fee was $1.50.[23]

During the first term Regina took English 101, French 101, Chemistry 101, and Mathematics 101. Students then completed English 101, French 101, Chemistry 101, and Mathematics 101 for the second term; for the final academic term Regina took Mathematics 101, Biology 101, French 101, Economics, and an elective course.

All students enrolled at the university were expected to reside in the dormitories. Regina resided in one of two female dorms for freshmen and sophomores. Arnett Hall was "well equipped, lighted by both gas and electricity, and heated by steam." Kezia Emery Hall[24] "was completed in 1913, at a cost of nearly $50,000, including furnishings and fixtures." It was "an attractive building in the colonial style, supplied with all modern conveniences, heated by hot water and lighted by electricity and gas." The dorms had "laundries, kitchens, and dining rooms . . . parlors and reception rooms."[25]

Every day at 11:45 Regina had to attend services in the Chapel that consisted of reading the Scripture, singing, and praying. There was a student prayer meeting every Wednesday evening, and Regina was required to attend church on the Sabbath.

The university recorded any unexcused absences either from class or religious exercises. If absences were excessive, parents or guardians were notified, and the student was encouraged to withdraw from the university. Regina had to observe all of the study hours and could not have visitors during this time. Students were responsible for any misconduct that occurred in their rooms in the residence halls, which also had to be clean and neat. Defacement of campus property was also not allowed, nor was littering or throwing trash outside of windows.

Regina had to adhere to a strict dress code, which specified: "Every girl must have rain coat, rubbers, umbrellas, and stout shoes for winter. Plain skirt and shirt waists or simple dresses should be provided. Elaborate apparel and costly jewelry are inappropriate and their use will not be permitted."

Students could not interact with the opposite sex without permission. Students also could not marry without permission. Regina could not possess immoral books or papers, intoxicating drinks or tobacco, or firearms or other deadly weapons. Gambling, profanity, and obscene behaviors were prohibited. Students were not allowed to leave campus without permission—even to visit their families. In addition to following all of the rules, the students had to observe the rules with "cheerful obedience."

Regina almost certainly chafed under the rules. *Arc of Justice* author Kevin Boyle, who wrote about another Wilberforce student, Ossian Sweet, noted that there were better African American schools, such as Fisk, Atlanta University, Lincoln University, and Howard. Boyle said that, "Graduates of those schools thought of Wilberforce as a backwater, provincial and pedestrian, and many of its students as earnest but utterly unsophisticated, well-meaning but not necessarily well educated."[26] A future acquaintance of Regina, W. E. B. Du Bois, worked there briefly and was not impressed.[27] Perhaps these are some of the reasons that Regina did not stay to complete her education at Wilberforce after coming from the sophisticated city of Chicago and maybe feeling out of place in the small town where the university was located. Throughout her life, Regina said virtually nothing about her experiences at Wilberforce or why she left.

While Regina was enrolled, after perceived abuse of privileges, the Board of Trustees asked President Scarborough to reinstate rules that would once again restrict fraternization among male and female students. Reaction was negative, dramatic, and swift. The students protested:

> One morning in May, barbed wire entanglements barricaded all the entrances to classroom buildings, and pickets lined the walks. Students were forbidden to leave their dormitories and violence was resorted to in several instances where attempts were made to attend classes. The law enforcement officials of Xenia were called upon for aid, but fully 600 male students could not be arrested and incarcerated. Late in the day, President Scarborough announced that for the present the old rule would not be carried out, and the strikers went quietly back to school.[28]

Conceivably this restrictive atmosphere was the reason that Regina left Wilberforce. We could speculate that she thought all of these rules were ridiculous, or perhaps she was part of the protest and was suspended or expelled, despite reports that indicated only male students were involved in the disturbance.

Whatever the cause, Regina left and returned to Chicago. Her refusal to return to Wilberforce may have also been prompted by problems at home. Later that summer, in August 1920, the *Chicago Defender* reported that her sister, fifteen-year-old Mercedes, "was taken to the Psychopathic hospital for observation, as it is feared by her relatives that her mind has become unbalanced."[29] A week later a second item appeared under the headline, "Diagnosis Proved False" and stated, "upon examination it was found that her ailment was merely due to nervousness." Was this item dissembling from the family or by the newspaper worried about incurring the wrath of her father, by then a famous attorney?[30] When classes resumed at Wilberforce, Regina remained in Chicago.

Using her Hyde Park High School and Wilberforce University library experience, Regina applied for a job at the Chicago Public Library. The institution was advertising for people to fill positions. In an article, "Being a Librarian," the unidentified author extolled the virtues of librarianship as a career—for young women. The author argued, "The difference between being a librarian and 'working in a library' is not one of position but of attitude—a state of mind." The library had positions for one hundred *women* "of the right kind" in its next training class and offered free instruction "in the fundamentals of library methods and practice" and a salary of $65 a month for a forty- to forty-four-hour work week.[31] The only requirement was a high-school degree for admission into the training class—which Regina more than fulfilled with one year of college under her belt.

The Chicago Public Library hired its staff through Chicago's Civil Service Commission—a lucky break for Regina. A person interested in working for one of Chicago's public institutions would present herself for the Civil Service test, which was given several times throughout the year. The test was graded, and if she scored high enough she would be considered an eligible candidate for a position and her name would be added to the bottom of the list. Chicago instituted the Civil Service exam system around 1895, most likely to prevent politicians (for example, aldermen, mayors, and judges) from telling the librarian—in this case—Carl Roden, to hire their son, niece, neighbor, or campaign contributor. There are dozens of letters in the Chicago Public Library's Special Collections and Preservation Division to Roden requesting such favors, with Roden replying that his hands were tied. The Civil Service test inadvertently resulted in fair hiring practices for African Americans—although this was most likely not its main intention.[32] Like her father, many decades earlier, Regina was able to overcome any possible prejudice about her race by obtaining a job through an examination system. The Chicago Civil Service Commission process required the following: "Applicants were in each case permitted to prepare a thesis, in their accompanying it by a certified record of experience and training, all of which was mailed to the Commission and became the basis of a rating determined by members of our own staff."[33] The reason for the exams were stated: "The precedent established by this wise and liberal method of holding civil service examinations will be most valuable and far-reaching in our plans for recruiting a staff numerically adequate and professionally competent to meet the requirements of our ever-increasing and expanding opportunities for service."[34]

In spite of Chicago's notorious reputation for corruption, the Chicago Public Library did not bow to political pressure.[35] Library director Roden's archives contain "letters protesting the assignment of 'colored' staff in White neighborhoods."[36] Carl Roden worked at the Chicago Public Library from 1886 when he started as a sixteen-year-old library page until 1950 when he retired as the chief librarian. He had served in that position since 1918 after the untimely death of his predecessor, Henry E. Legler, who died after only eight years in office. Legler is credited with the construction of the regional library branch system (there had been only one branch when he came into office), but Roden continued his work.[37]

On August 17, 1921, Roden received a list of eligible candidates for Junior Library Assistant (JLA) positions from City Hall. Roden had forty-one JLA positions to fill. At the top of the list was Regina M. Anderson of 530 E. 45th Street. She was hired in August 1921 at Grade 2, Junior Library Assistant, at a salary of $780 a year.

The month that Regina was hired, August 1921, revealed that the number of books circulated for home use in all the branches equaled 509,900.[38] The number of new and renewed library cards equaled 5,178. The Chicago Public Library had a total of 1,092,240 volumes.[39]

Regina worked for the Chicago Public Library for only a brief period. In June 1922, she was granted a leave of absence "not to exceed thirty days."[40] However, an examination of the 1921 annual report might reveal why she left. During 1921, "nineteen branches were ordered closed and service hours in the remaining branches and in the Central Library were curtailed. A reduction in staff by the dismissal of 100 persons . . . omission of considerable repairs and renovations of . . . buildings and equipment." However, "It affords a slight measure of gratification to be able to conclude this chronicle of misfortune with the statement that the institution has now weathered the storm and closes the year without serious liabilities." The report also indicated that there were "suspensions of all automatic increases in salary."[41] Maybe the atmosphere that Regina encountered during her first year discouraged her and she began to consider finding a job in a more economically stable environment. She was among "the scanty personnel in the surviving branches [who] . . . struggled valiantly through the year to deal with the evergrowing demands of constituencies."[42] Not only were staff members overworked, but apparently they were underpaid too. "The scale of library salaries, never high, has now fallen so far below that in kindred lines," the report cited, "we can no longer stem the tide of defections."[43] Roden had long noticed that the library had great difficulty hiring trained library staff because Chicago lacked a library school and "graduates of other schools are so quickly snapped up by other cities with better salary offers and more elastic employment conditions."[44] Eventually, the University of Chicago would offer a degree in librarianship. Further, Roden noted that, "The revision of the salary schedules is an urgent necessity. . . . The present scale . . . is totally inadequate and beneath contempt."[45]

Regina never returned to work at the Chicago Public Library. The October 23, 1922, Proceedings of the Board of Directors noted that Regina M. Anderson resigned her position on September 10, 1922.[46] This date was clearly more than thirty days after her request for a leave of absence in June. Her not honoring her request would come back to haunt her.

Regina's experiences at the Chicago Public Library were not all negative. She later said she was influenced by librarian Vivian G. Harsh. After graduating from Chicago's Wendell Phillips High School, Harsh went to work at the Chicago Public Library in 1909 as a junior clerk. She never worked anywhere else. After attending library school at Boston's Simmons College, she became a head librarian in 1924 and "succeeded in building one of the most important research collections on black history and literature in the United

States."[47] The current Vivian G. Harsh Collection of Afro-American History and Literature at the Carter G. Woodson Regional Library of the Chicago Public Library is named after her.[48]

Around this time Regina's youngest sister, Mercedes, died at age eighteen. Regina would say that her sister died from a broken heart over the end of her parents' marriage. Given the earlier news reports of mental instability and hospitalization in a psychopathic hospital, it is possible that she committed suicide. Her family would not talk about her death in detail. However, Regina would later tell her great-niece Angelina that Mercedes "died suddenly and not from an illness."[49] No death certificate has been located in Cook County records. If Regina's relatives are correct about Mercedes's death at age eighteen, that would mean she died in 1923, which became a pivotal time in Regina's life, a possible impetus for her to start over in New York City to escape the memories of her sister's death back home in Chicago.

Regina was determined to stay in New York where she was told by the New York Public Library administrator, "To us you're not American. You're not white."

3. Harlem Renaissance Women and 580 St. Nicholas Avenue

When Regina's interviewer at the New York Public Library told her that she was not American, Regina recalled that she was "quite startled because I never had this confrontation in Chicago." With fewer African Americans in Chicago than in New York City, the Chicago Public Library hired more African Americans to work in its libraries as a result of the civil service system, which hired and placed people based upon their scores on the exam regardless of race.[1]

Her New York Public Library interviewer concluded, "Because of your color . . . we'll have to send you to Harlem to work." He assumed Regina knew Harlem and asked whether she had a place there. She replied that she "hadn't been to Harlem," because she "hadn't had occasion to go up there." Regina's job at the New York Public Library was actually not her first in New York City. She took a job briefly in the Womrath Rental Library, an experience she said she "liked very much [because the work was] . . . quite different from [that of] a public library."[2] Rental libraries flourished during the 1920s through the 1940s. By 1935, there were about 50,000 nationwide. Most were located in drugstores, card stores, and gift shops and rented both fiction and nonfiction, although most emphasized fiction because public libraries often frowned upon patrons reading too much fiction: "The larger rental libraries . . . were exhorted to have a library clerk or two with a friendly extroverted character who enjoyed reading and who followed book reviews. The 'librarian' should be someone who was good at chatting about books with patrons and willing to recommend selections."[3] While working at Womrath, Regina took a vacation, which included a sightseeing trip to Boston, and applied for a job at NYPL upon her return to the city.

At the time, Regina resided in the YWCA near the 42nd Street Branch in midtown Manhattan and not at the YWCA in Harlem, where most African Americans found a place to stay when they arrived in New York City.[4] Either Regina was unfamiliar with this practice, or she felt at home in the non–African American YWCA. It's possible the proprietors did not know that she was not white. Her NYPL interviewer suggested that she "find a friend" to live with in Harlem. She called her married friend Inez Wilson, who had a first-floor apartment where Regina could live.

In Wil Haygood's biography of the boxer Sugar Ray Robinson he described two types of Harlems inhabited by African Americans. Robinson's family lived on the side that was "darker and unforgiving . . . a rough place, a lower-class enclave of broken families, of flophouses and boardinghouses. Of racketeers and gangsters, of big crime and petty crime. Of handouts and hand-me-down clothing, of little boys often scampering about like lambs being hunted."[5] In the other Harlem, wrote Haygood, "[T]here were poetry readings and social teas; there were gatherings that featured notable speakers who talked about national affairs and the doings they were privy to in the Roosevelt White House. . . . In this Harlem there was music by the Harlem Symphony; there were NAACP galas and fraternity soirees. . . . That was the bright side of the two-sided coin of Harlem." This was the Harlem that Regina and the friends she made through the library inhabited. They were not that interested in events in the other Harlem, such as the political movement of Marcus Garvey, the controversial leader of the Universal Negro Improvement Association (UNIA). Regina and her circle could not help but notice the "parades of the Garvey Movement, but most of our group just laughed at the idea. . . . [W]e didn't know the real significance of it. . . . [W]e were too busy living our lives and . . . being interested in the . . . movement . . . [w]hich they now call the [Harlem] Renaissance."[6]

Events collided to put Regina at the forefront of the Harlem Renaissance, a cultural movement marked by increased literary, musical, and artistic creativity by African American artists who wanted to challenge the prevailing stereotypical representation of their image. Writers and artists came from all over the United States to participate. In Los Angeles, writer Wallace Thurman encouraged fellow post-office worker Arna Bontemps to go to Harlem. *Opportunity* editor Charles S. Johnson encouraged Zora Neale Hurston to move to New York City. All of these great thinkers, writers, and artists would pass through the 135th Street Branch, where Regina was assigned.

When Regina applied for a job at NYPL, less than half of 1 percent of the country's librarians were African American.[7] The 135th Street Branch first opened in 1905 and, reflecting the neighborhood, approximately 95 percent of the patrons were white. By 1920, at the end of the Great Migration, the community was split with about 50 percent whites and 50 percent African Americans. Three years later, around the time Regina started to work at the branch, eighty percent of the patrons were African American. African Americans flocked to Harlem from lower Manhattan neighborhoods and from the southern states as the Jewish and Italian populations left Harlem to relocate to Queens and the Bronx.[8] Historian Jonathan Gill attributed this increase to many things, including an accessible "subway line and the expiration of many racial housing covenants" that had prevented African Americans from renting in the neighborhood. There had even been opposition to "policy changes that allowed Negroes to use the New York Public Library branch at 103 West 135th Street."[9]

By the time Regina arrived the branch had become the de facto "colored branch" of the New York Public Library. Supervising the 135th Street Branch was legendary librarian Ernestine Rose (1880–1961), an outspoken white advocate for the African Americans it served.[10] Rose protested the designation of her branch as the "colored" one. She believed that African American librarians should be able to work at any of the NYPL branches and did not have to serve only African American patrons. She hired white library assistants too, because she thought it would benefit the white librarians and the patrons to be served by an interracial staff.[11]

Although Regina did not like being pigeonholed and relegated to the Harlem Branch of the NYPL because of her race, working there as a substitute librarian got her foot in the door of the larger institution. She accepted the position of junior clerk at the 135th Street Branch, at Grade 1, beginning in April of 1923.[12] Regina was Promoted to Grade 2, based upon her previous library experiences at Hyde Park High School, Wilberforce, and the Chicago Public Library. She earned $102.41 per month beginning in January of 1924.[13] This was a significant increase from the $65 per month she earned at the Chicago Public Library.

During the year that Regina started working at the 135th Street Branch, the Circulation Department was concerned about the quality of the books in the branches, which were badly worn and depleted. They were also concerned about the impact of the advent of radio on "reading for recreation."[14] Possibly affecting circulation figures was the new policy of allowing patrons to check out a maximum of two books of fiction to encourage them to read more "educational" fare like nonfiction books. The head of the circulation department of the New York Public Library was in charge of administering the branches, and a large section of her 1924 Director's Report was devoted to praising the 135th Street Branch:

Relations between practically all the Branch Libraries and the several communities are close and important, but those developed in the last few years between the 135th Street Branch and the Negro Community in Harlem are particularly interesting and effective. The Branch Librarian belongs to many neighborhood social groups; she has arranged monthly Book Evenings attracting a large number of people to hear literary personages; she has arranged a weekly Forum for the discussion of current topics, and has been closely associated with what promises to be a valuable Community Theater Movement, which originated with meetings held in the branch. A dramatic director has been chosen, and the movement is to include extensive class work and many groups. The Branch Library assembly room will be used as one of the centers for class work and for production on a small scale.[15]

Specific aspects of Regina's day-to-day activities at the branch are unknown but, generally, new assistants spent a day training at the Interbranch Loan Office. They studied, "book ordering, cataloguing, binding, mending, and discarding" books. They also toured various departments in the main library at 42nd Street and Fifth Avenue.[16]

Regina enthusiastically supported Rose in her community outreach activities, including organizing the North Harlem Community Forum, which took place during the 1920s. The forum's activities were literary, cerebral, and often controversial and were noted in the "Library Notes" section of the *New York Amsterdam News*, and sometimes in the *Pittsburgh Courier*.[17] Noted journalist and satirist George Schuyler chaired the committee[18] and members included Rose, Regina, and Elise McDougald, who would go on to write the essay "The Task of Negro Womanhood" in the groundbreaking *New Negro* anthology. Lectures covered subjects such as "philosophy, war, peace, journalism, labor, psychology, sociology, economics, militarism, literature, poetry, race relations, etc."[19] The goal of the forum was to "make Harlem a more intellectual place to live in" by bringing in "some noted speaker or scholar, . . . on subjects both timely and vital to the educational advancement of the community."[20] For example, W. E. B. Du Bois spoke about his experiences with people in West Africa and their negative perceptions of "American Negroes."

The forum educated its audiences on a wide variety of social, political, historical, and literary topics and brought Regina into an important hub of intellectual life in New York City. At one forum, Margaret Sanger announced, "American women are divided into two classes . . . those who have birth control and those who have not. Rich women can get all the knowledge on this subject they want, and if it is good for them it is also good for the poor, who cannot afford to rear large families, like the rich." (Police officers stood by in case she attempted to distribute birth control literature.) The West Indian public intellectual and writer Hubert Harrison hosted sessions to celebrate the anniversary of Lewis Carroll's birth and later presented "The Writings of Sir Arthur Conan Doyle" at the forum. With lectures and talks on "The Social and Political Outlook of India," "Race Prejudice," "Racial Aspects of Labor Conditions in Latin America," and "Ghandi and the Present Situation in India," the forum became the city's premier stage for discussions about racism. After Columbia University professor and anthropologist Franz Boas (later a mentor of Zora Neale Hurston) spoke at the forum, the *New Amsterdam News* headline read, "Race Superiority Bunk, Says Boas." The journalist noted that Boas "has done more than any other in the United States to destroy the theory of race superiority. In his address, he said that there is no evidence whatever to prove that the white man is inherently superior to any other, or that the Negro would not have accomplished all the white race has if it had been placed in the same environment or had the same opportunities."[21]

Theophilus Lewis, a theater critic and writer, wrote, "The credit for a great deal of the success achieved [by the forums] this season is due Miss Regina M. Anderson . . . who has largely directed and executed the difficult tasks of publicity and finance."[22] An example of Regina's efforts appears in letters to journalist and editor Joseph Freeman, an early proponent of Marxism and Communism. She wrote to him:

> Perhaps you will remember I mentioned tentative plans concerning our Forum to you some time ago. Since then we have weathered a rather successful period of about four months. We are now arranging our spring schedules. I would be very grateful if you would speak for us perhaps on April 22nd on some subject of interest to you, perhaps—"American Imperialism" or "Anatole France." . . . Your interests are all rather varied, but so very well worth while [*sic*].

She also used her connections and social grace to further develop the season's program, in this instance seeking Freeman's assistance to enlist former University of Pennsylvania professor Scott Nearing, who had been fired for speaking out against World War I, as a speaker for the forum:

> I am also writing Scott Nearing, hoping that he will consent to give a lecture for us on Socialism. I addressed my letter to the Rand School. Do you think that perhaps his answer might be a bit more favorable if you spoke to him also for me?[23]

Regina publicized forum events by sending personal invitations, including the following to Freeman:

> Enclosed you will find an announcement of one of the coming lectures given under the auspices of the North Harlem Community Forum. This occasion

represents Mr. Kellogg's first formal appearance in Harlem since the recent number of the Survey-Graphic [edited by Alain Locke and later published as the *New Negro*]. We expect this to be one of our most interesting meetings during the season. I am sure that you will enjoy the discussion, meeting some of those who contributed to that particular number of the magazine. I would be quite pleased should you find it convenient to be present.[24]

These forums almost certainly inspired the lectures that Regina later scheduled at the 115th Street and Washington Heights Branches.[25]

In addition to connecting to leading writers, artists, and thinkers through her correspondence, Regina had occasion to meet many of the great minds of the Harlem Renaissance in person through her job at the 135th Street Branch. She "came in contact with a lot of the young writers who would come in there. She would arrange for space so they could write."[26] Regina would "set aside a small work area for African American artists in the library, and Langston Hughes, Eric Walrond, and Claude McKay were among its users."[27] Poet/writer and later librarian Arna Bontemps described his arrival in New York City and his first encounter with the 135th Street Branch: "After I found a room, I went out to see what Harlem was like, . . . to start watching for the public library. . . . And when I got there, there were a couple of very nice-looking girls sitting at the desk, colored girls. I had never seen that before, you know, in California."[28] As he completed an application for a library card, one of the librarians, Roberta Bosley, a cousin of poet Countee Cullen, recognized his name from the current issue of *Crisis*, where he had his writing published. Bontemps's search for the 135th Street Branch was a typical excursion of newly arrived artists and intellectuals to Harlem. Langston Hughes also wrote about his own introduction to Harlem. Like Bontemps, Hughes first secured a room at the YMCA and then went to the 135th Street Branch library where he encountered Ernestine Rose and Catherine Latimer, the first African American NYPL librarian. He described Latimer as a "luscious café au lait."[29]

Regina worked with Latimer, who headed the Division of Negro Literature, History, and Prints until NYPL purchased the collection compiled by bibliophile Arturo Schomburg (1874–1938) and named him the head of that division. Latimer also created the clipping files about various aspects of African American life that remain an important reference resource. Regina also briefly joined African American librarian Sarah Peterson Delaney (1889–1958) at the 135th Street Branch. Delaney left in 1924 to assume a position at Tuskegee Institute, where she developed her specialty in bibliotherapy—literally therapy through books—which she used to help WWI African American veterans deal with what is now known as post traumatic stress disorder (PTSD).

It is not known how Regina and Ethel Ray Nance became friends, but they probably knew several people in common and each had a need for a roommate. They ended up living at 580 St. Nicholas Avenue with a third young woman named Louella Tucker in an apartment they called "Dream Haven."[30] This address was "[o]ne of Harlem's swankiest apartment buildings, high on 'Sugar Hill' (where affluent and prominent Afro-Americans were increasingly settling)."[31] It faced the green lawns of City College. In Carl Van Vechten's *Nigger Heaven* [a novel believed by many to be largely based on Dream Haven], the apartment is described as "an apartment on the sixth storey of a building on Edgecombe Avenue, that pleasant thoroughfare facing the rocky cliff surmounted by City College."[32] The novelist brought himself infamy with his book, but he left what is probably a good picture of Dream Haven in his description of Mary the librarian's apartment:

> Each of the girls had her own bedroom; the use of the sitting-room they shared. The sitting-room, though small, was pleasant. The furniture included an up-holstered couch, several easy chairs, a desk, a table with an electric lamp, and a phonograph. Blue-flowered chintz curtains hung at the window. The walls were brightened by framed reproductions of paintings by Bellini and Carpaccio which Mary had collected during a journey through Italy.[33]

One bedroom, seemingly Regina's, was described as more "sober. There was only one picture in her room, a reproduction of the Monna [*sic*] Lisa. Her bed-cover was plain white: her dressing-table austere and generally devoid of articles, save for inexpensive brush, comb, and mirror." Its bookshelves contained the types of books that we could imagine that Regina also read, for example, those by Aldous Huxley and Sherwood Anderson. This character also had many autographed books by "Negro" writers including Charles W. Chestnutt, James Weldon Johnson, Jean Toomer, Claude McKay, W. E. B. Du Bois, Walter White, and Jessie Fauset, many of Regina's personal friends. Along with the books, "on her writing-table stood a photograph of her father, in a silver frame."[34] Regina adored her father and was proud to be his daughter. News articles about Regina often noted that she hailed from Chicago, where her father was a celebrated defense attorney.

Regina, Ethel, and Louella were among "some of the first Negroes who moved into that building. It had been a totally white occupied building when we moved in there."[35] Academy Award nominee Ethel Waters "lived across the hall from us," Ethel later recalled.[36] Waters was not part of Regina's social world according to Ethel who "only met her on the elevator or coming in and out of the building."[37] When Ethel's father noticed Waters's name and the name of a man with a different last name listed on their apartment door and questioned her about their living arrangements, Ethel pleaded ignorance. Although the trio did not hang out in Waters's social circle, Waters's presence in the building no doubt added a touch of glamour to their lives.

Like Regina, Ethel Ray was raised in the Midwest, the daughter of a doting African American father and activist. As president of the local NAACP, William H. Ray "invited [W. E. B.] Du Bois to speak at a chapter meeting,"[38] which led to "a special 43-year relationship" between Ethel and Du Bois. Ray took his daughter with him on an extraordinary four-month cross-country train ride to meet with African American leaders. At the National Urban League conference in Kansas City she met Charles S. Johnson, editor of the League's organ *Opportunity*. Returning to Minnesota, Ethel became the first African American stenographer in the Minnesota Legislature. she recalled, "I got newspaper publicity as being the first Black stenographer and the different organizations were very kind about—about giving little teas and luncheons for me. And I started getting letters, the information had been reproduced in other Negro papers."[39] That's how she "got the offer of a job in Kansas City from the Urban League."[40] "And while I was working in Kansas City," Ethel reflected, "I got the offer from Charles Johnson to come to New York to work on *Opportunity*."[41] *Opportunity* was a magazine that "promoted socialist philosophies and advanced its theories for racial uplift and success."[42] The idea of going to New York City was too appealing for Ethel to turn down.

Regina had much in common with Ethel, including being a novice at New York City life. At 580 they learned together "about the little things about New York such as you tipped your elevator man, you tipped the doorman, because . . . these little acts . . . helped towards your security. They would accept packages for you."[43] Regina's friend and roommate described herself as "being above the average sized person."[44] Indeed, in pictures Ethel towered over the other people regardless of gender. She thought that she and the petite Regina "complemented each other."[45] The third roommate, Louella Tucker, has been described as "a goodtime girl" and Ethel confessed that, "we needed her for the rent." Their rent "was high, even divided three ways. Salaries were paid monthly, and [we] frequently found our food money almost exhausted before the end of four weeks."[46] Louella worked as a typist at *Opportunity* and that is where Ethel most likely encountered her.[47]

Together with the *Messenger*, published by A. Phillip Randolph and Chandler Owen, and the *Crisis*, published by the NAACP, *Opportunity* was one of the three most popular African American magazines.[48] Du Bois had twice asked Ethel to work for him on the *Crisis*, but she was detained by her mother's illness.[49] Ethel recalled, "Dr. Du Bois would tease me and say 'you came to New York to work for . . . uh . . . rival magazine.'"[50] Her parents were not happy about her going so far away from home but they "knew that Dr. Du Bois was there and he felt that though his friendship with him, I would have a degree of guardianship."[51]

Through her roommate, Regina came to know Du Bois—and managed to eat very well on her librarian's salary. Ethel recalled:

> Dr. Du Bois . . . used to take us to dinner. We three girls who lived together were only paid once a month. Our salaries weren't large and we paid $85 a month rent and that was a great deal for the three of us. So toward the end of the month usually that last week we would call him and ask him how he was, if he was in town, and he would say, I presume you're hungry. [Laughter] Then he would take us out to dinner. He was very nice about that. He got quite a kick out of us.[52]

On some Saturday afternoons Du Bois would drive Regina and her roommates upstate and serve them sandwiches and coffee from a thermos that he would bring with him. Another time he took the young women to Coney Island where they had, "[c]ourse after course, starting with shrimp cocktail, oysters, other fish common to the Eastern seaboard, roasted corn in the husk and salad." Afterward, the trio "would be full to bursting. He laughed as we slowed down toward the end of the sumptuous feast. 'Now I hope I've filled you up!' At the moment we felt as though we wouldn't require nourishment for weeks, perhaps even a month."[53]

Du Bois liked hanging out with the trio of young women. "[I]t seemed he enjoyed our adventurousness and spontaneity," recalled Ethel. "We were always doing something, having people at the apartment, meeting new people."[54] Their lack of funds did not prevent Regina and her roommates from hosting guests: "The summer after we acquired the new apartment all three of us had visitors from far away places, who wanted to come to New York now that they had friends there! Our budget suffered, naturally, as well as our rest. But too much entertainment wasn't expected of us, since there were enough things to do in the city for visitors to find for themselves."[55]

Regina and Ethel reinforced each other's acquaintances and friendships with the who's who of the Harlem Renaissance. Ethel worked for *Opportunity* as an executive secretary from 1924 until 1926. She performed a variety of tasks and functioned "as managing editor of *Opportunity*. She wrote news items, screened manuscript submissions, and read proofs."[56] She also worked as a "talent scout" for Charles Johnson by introducing him to "promising new books," writers, etc. No doubt Regina, who met many of these writers at the library, and Ethel shared information on their respective projects and people they knew. According to Ethel, James Weldon Johnson, coauthor of the Black National Anthem "Lift Every Voice and Sing," "and his wife were close friends of Regina's."[57] But Ethel herself met Johnson when she delivered manuscripts to him for an *Opportunity* literary contest.

Ethel noted, "with Regina in the library, it gave us access to a lot of people. . . . [T]hey really used our home if there was some people in town because we could get a group together very quickly" for a party or a reading.[58] Ethel's job at the Urban League also gave her a chance to meet artists because, "Charles S. Johnson was quite accessible and liked 'new finds.'"[59] Through her librarian position, Regina "had many first hand meetings with local and out of town artists at the library"[60] and she "came in contact with all these people. . . . Some writers were very fortunate being associated with her. And, she worked very hard. She would bring home seven or eight books at night as these new books came out. She (would) digest enough to give some kind of short review for the next day" for her job.[61] Similarly, the character of Mary Love in the novel *Nigger Heaven*, whom some believe was inspired by Regina,[62] is described as having "a row of a dozen or so of the latest books which she had borne home from the library in an effort to keep abreast with the best of the modern output, an altruistic endeavor which enabled her to offer her patrons advice when they were in doubt, as so often she found they were."[63] When the novelist describes a tough day at work for Mary, we can imagine Regina having a similar response: "An hour later she felt she couldn't bear it if she had another inquiry for A. S. M. Hutchinson or Zane Grey. She made it a point of honour to try to encourage the young patrons of the library to improve their taste in reading. . . . Patiently, for the tenth time within the hour she recommended Jean Toomer's *Cane*." And later, Mary says, "I'm getting so tired of handing out trash that I'm in a frightfully bad temper."[64]

Regina found an outlet for any bad temper in the salon that she and Ethel created for artists and intellectuals. Regina did not describe her day-to-day life as a librarian in any published accounts, but Mary Love's life may offer some insight into Regina's:

> Mary's life was simple but full; she found she had very little time to spare. Six days a week, and one evening, she worked in the library. Leaving the library usually in the afternoon around five, she often went to the Park for a walk. Then she came home, changed her dress, and read and mended her clothes while Olive [believed to be based in part on Ethel] cooked dinner. In the evening, frequently there would be callers: the girls knew all the young men and women in the Harlem literary circles, most of the young school-teachers, doctors, lawyers, and dentists.[65]

Guests at 580 were a who's who of the Harlem Renaissance: artists, poets, writers, songwriters, intellectuals, and activists. The Sugar Hill apartment "served as a sort of Renaissance USO, offering a couch, a meal, sympathy, and proper introduction to wicked Harlem for newcomers on the Urban League approved list."[66] In 1924, *Opportunity* editor Charles S. Johnson suggested that Zora Neale Hurston contact his assistant Ethel on her arrival in New York, assuring Hurston that she would be warmly welcomed at her apartment. Hurston ended up staying on a couch at 580 St. Nicholas Avenue when she arrived in New York City.[67] Ethel recollected, "Zora could tell a good story . . . pretended that she couldn't talk English and so she was passed off as an African and was permitted to stay at this hotel. It gave us a good laugh."[68] Later, "Zora was a person rather hard to keep within bounds, you had to ride herd on her a bit, so she stayed with us at the time. We felt responsible in making certain that she was going to keep these appointments [at Barnard College for a scholarship] because with her if something else interesting came up, off she was."[69]

Ethel recalled, "I would say that Countee Cullen used to drop by most frequently on his way home from school. We were right near City College. . . . He was always so unassuming and charming, a fine young man, and we were only too happy to have him come, whatever we were doing we would stop and listen to it."[70] Cullen was one of the most prolific Harlem Renaissance poets and was the editor of the poetry anthology *Caroling Dusk*. He won many literary prizes and wrote a column, "The Dark Tower," for *Opportunity*. Cullen was almost like a little brother to the trio at 580. They discovered that although he had written a poem about "beautiful brown girls dancing in a cabaret" that he had never actually been to a cabaret. The women "felt that his education had been neglected."[71] For his college graduation they took him to "our favorite one [cabaret] over on the upper Fifth Avenue down a flight from the street, which we had named the 'Cat on the Saxophone.' . . . He was delighted."[72] Ethel fondly recollected, "Yes, we knew Countee and we saw a great deal of him. . . . [H]e came by quite often to read parts of poems that he was in the process of writing. And he would come in and say, 'would you like to hear what I've written' or 'do you have time to listen to something that I've written.'" She said he wasn't "showing off being egotistic or grandstanding, it was just I think he appreciated our friendship."[73]

Cullen in turn brought Arna Bontemps to Regina's salon. Upon his arrival in Harlem, Bontemps contacted Cullen, who invited him to 580, telling him that Langston Hughes would be at the gathering.[74] Bontemps and Hughes became fast friends and went on to exchange over 2,300 letters between 1925 and 1967. In one 1962 letter, Bontemps recalled hearing Hughes read "to the group at Ethel Ray and Regina's apartment."[75] Hughes "was (a) very likeable sort of a person, very easy to know. . . . Someone asked whether he had done much writing (during his travels) and he reached in his inside pocket and pulled out a little notebook and read some of his poems"[76] to the group assembled at 580.

Regina's salon also helped cement the lifelong friendship between Hughes and the Iowa-born Carl Van Vechten, a writer and patron of the arts, and a supporter of African American artists during the Harlem Renaissance. Whereas Hughes was "likable" to Regina and Ethel, Van Vechten would not remain so. They felt that Van Vechten had exploited his insider knowledge of the African American upper-middle-class community in his 1926 novel, *Nigger Heaven*. Originally a regular guest at the salon (he had introduced to 580 Jean Toomer, author of the early Harlem Renaissance masterpiece *Cane*), Van Vechten made no more daybook entries about social engagements with the women of 580 after *Nigger Heaven* was published.

In any case, the third roommate, Louella Tucker, had been more likely than Regina and Ethel to socialize with Van Vechten and his good friend the West Indian journalist and writer Eric Walrond.[77]

Walrond was a frequent visitor to 580 and would regale the roommates with tales about his experiences with discrimination. The trio thought that "Eric went out to have these experiences and trying new things so he could write about them and have a new story, because each time that he would go some place in downtown New York and ran into discrimination, a splendid article would come out of the experience."[78] With his press pass, Walrond obtained tickets to cultural happenings and invited the trio from 580 to events at Carnegie Hall and an outdoor concert by Marian Anderson. Similarly, the fictional librarian Mary Love and her roommate were described as attending "good plays and musical entertainments, revues and song recitals alike, downtown, usually sitting in the balcony to save expense, although Olive was light enough and Mary's features were sufficiently Latin so that they were not rudely received when they asked at the box-office for places in the orchestra."[79]

As Regina's culinary and cultural life flourished despite her limited funds, so did her salon. Ethel Ray remembered:

> We couldn't do any lavish entertaining, but I think it was that the younger people who were starting to write and draw, it was a place where they could drop in and they could meet others and it was a place where whenever anyone had a little success, any kind of success, or they were published or they'd had an interview . . . we'd get together and everybody would rejoice . . . it was sort of a little family.[80]

Most of the gatherings at 580 revolved around the arts and sometimes around alcohol. Their social crowd "didn't have to rely on liquor for our comeuppance. We didn't have the money in the first place, but whatever spontaneity and fun that we had was certainly engendered, just from ourselves."[81] However, sometimes alcohol was served at 580. Ethel recalled:

> I remember Van Vechten coming into our apartment this one evening and inquiring who was the hostess, well, the girls didn't move, so I moved and he handed me this bottle of some exquisite wine. I took it to the kitchen, which was on the side of the living room and just left it there. Then later on when it was to be served, two of the women . . . their names escaped me not entirely, but we'll just skip that, refused it when we passed the wine glasses. And then almost immediately, they came out in the kitchen and asked, "may we have some" and I said "no, [laughing] if you're not willing to accept it in front of the group, I'm sorry."[82]

Michael A. Lerner's book about prohibition in New York City, *Dry Manhattan*, included a chapter, "Hootch Joints in Harlem." Drinking could be found among all classes of African American people. He said that there were generally two views about drinking among African Americans in Harlem: "a traditional generation of post-Reconstruction leaders, who saw in Prohibition an opportunity for blacks to prove themselves as citizens, and a younger generation, more attuned to modern urban culture, who embraced the cultural rebellion of the Prohibition era as a sign of a less moralistic and possibly more tolerant nation."[83] No doubt Regina and her social group belonged to the latter. The older generation thought that Prohibition could help the image of the African American in terms of respectability—a conundrum most likely faced by the young women who wanted to imbibe but did not want to do so publicly. Lerner described writer Dorothy West's observations:

> "Respectable types" and Harlem's well-to-do were enthusiastically joining the drinking culture. At one cocktail party, West recalled, professors, heirs and heiresses, and college-educated professionals from "good families" were all "lapping up" their hostess's liquor without reservation. West's recollections indicated that within the world of Harlem society, the desire to appear "smart" and sophisticated had replaced concern for respectability and moral righteousness.[84]

Lerner also stated that "the city's African-American middle class came to accept drinking, partaking in the thrills of nightlife, and jazz culture as badges of urban sophistication." Lerner concluded, "Prohibition enforcement failed as drastically in Harlem as it did in every other section of the city."[85]

The salon at 580 was a fixture of a social circuit that included numerous other happenings. Regina's socialite friend A'Lelia Walker (heiress of Madame C. J. Walker, the self-made hair products millionaire) threw parties that were arguably more famous or infamous than Regina's. A'Lelia Walker opened her home on W. 136th Street as a grand, elaborate salon called "The Dark Tower." In characteristically charming response to excess, Regina presented Walker's affianced daughter with the gift of books at a prewedding party.[86]

Prior to Van Vechten's ostracism from their salon, Regina and Ethel also attended his parties, which Ethel described as "bohemian." She recalled, we "went to one gathering in his apartment and I remember cats, they had a large, large number of cats and they had beautiful pictures and it was a very graceful, luxurious place as I remember it."[87] In general Ethel did not like to go to parties at the Van Vechten's or "downtown"—code word for parties held by white people, whom she felt "just liked to be able to say [they] knew Negroes."[88] But she did attend a party, probably with Regina, for Countee Cullen in "Boni & Liveright's penthouse on top of the publishing house."[89] She recalled, "It was so strange stopping in front of this office building which was all dark, but the penthouse, on the roof, was the scene of the party. And it was a lovely, lovely affair."[90] Albert and Charles Boni and their partner Horace Liveright were known for quality publishing of African American writers' books. Their firm was responsible for publishing Jean Toomer's *Cane* and Jessie Fauset's first novel, *There Is Confusion*.[91]

Fauset has often been referred to as the "midwife" of the Harlem Renaissance for her work as a mentor to the younger generation. Both Regina and Ethel attended functions of the Professional Women's Luncheon Club.[92] Ethel recalled that Fauset was "one of the more conventional people, although she didn't seem to frown on some of the . . . uh . . . well we'll coin the word 'outwardness' of some of the other people."[93] Unlike Walker's Dark Tower parties, at Fauset's Sunday afternoon teas "there was a certain decorum when you entered her house."[94]

Fauset was also one of the Harlem Renaissance's most productive novelists. To celebrate the publication of her novel *There Is Confusion*, Regina and Ethel helped Charles S. Johnson plan a Civic Club *Opportunity* dinner with Fauset as the guest of honor on March 21, 1924. The list of invitees included W. E. B. Du Bois, James Weldon Johnson, Jean Toomer, Countee Cullen, Langston Hughes, and Claude McKay. Ironically, Fauset's accomplishment was overshadowed by the wealth of talent that gathered in her honor. Many credit the dinner with launching the Harlem Renaissance by giving African American writers and poets an opportunity to showcase their work before prospective publishers, magazine editors, and patrons. The event prompted Paul Kellogg, editor-in-chief of the *Survey Graphic*, a progressive magazine, to devote an entire issue to the output of African American artists and intellectuals. Noted philosopher and Howard University professor, as well as the dinner's master of ceremonies,

Alain Locke, compiled and edited the special issue, titled *Harlem: Mecca of the New Negro*. It introduced the general public to Harlem Renaissance poets, writers, visual artists, and intellectuals and would later be published as the groundbreaking *New Negro Anthology*. Thus, Fauset's book party became one of the pivotal events in Harlem Renaissance history.

This compilation of the *Survey Graphic*'s special issue also had a connection with 580. Ethel remembered, "There were two or three meetings that I find recorded in my diary when people from the *Survey* came to Harlem and they came to our apartment for a part of their conferences."[95] Carl Van Doren and James Weldon Johnson attended some of the meetings in 580 to discuss the issue. The German-born artist Winhold Reiss attended one of the meetings and wanted suggestions for people from different professions to include in the issue. Reiss provided many illustrations for the *New Negro*, with portraits that showed African Americans as dignified subjects.

After the Civic Club dinner, and a stop at Small's Cabaret, many of the participants wandered over to 580 for an afterparty. Ethel reminisced, "it was after this affair that a number of them went up to our apartment, after we had gone to a Cabaret, and then we went to our apartment where we usually wound up and had bacon and eggs, that was our standard food we had on hand all the time."[96] (The trio were not exactly good cooks and they likely offered this limited fare because that's all they could cook.) "We went up on the roof the next morning and took some pictures," Ethel remembered.[97] One of the most famous Harlem Renaissance photographs shows five handsome, highly accomplished African American men dressed in suits: from left to right, Langston Hughes, Charles S. Johnson, E. Franklin Frazier, Rudolph Fisher, and Hubert Delany. Frazier was a noted sociologist most well-known for his publication *Black Bourgeoisie*. Fisher is often named as one of the first African American mystery writers for his novel, *The Conjure Man Dies*. Delany followed several of his siblings (including the famous Delany sisters)[98] to Harlem and went on to become a judge.

The photographs taken at 580 the morning after the party document young friendships that anchored the Harlem Renaissance and would last throughout the lives of the guests and their hostesses. In another photograph, Delany (who would later be a member of Regina's wedding party) stands next to his future bride, Clarissa Scott, whose poems were published in *Caroling Dusk*, *Opportunity*, and the *Crisis*. Ethel stands next to Langston Hughes and sisters of Jessie Fauset and Dr. Rudolph Fisher. In the front row, Esther Popel, another *Crisis* and *Opportunity* poet, stands next to "a very delicate little person,"[99] their hostess Regina Anderson.

Scholar Kathleen Pfeiffer has described the librarian character in *Nigger Heaven* as "a cultured, intellectual and race-conscious librarian, [who] maintains the sort of conservative, Victorian sensibility which racially progressive black readers appreciated."[100] However, Pfeiffer writes, "Mary defies easy categorization, as she simultaneously lauds the African and African American art, writing, and music that drew white America's attention to Harlem."[101] Regina embodied these traits and in her job as a librarian she brought African American writers and artists to the attention of Harlem's residents. In 1926, her dear friend Ethel Ray returned to Minnesota to care for her sick mother. She was not forgotten, as Langston Hughes reassured her in 1932, when he asked: "What made you think I could have forgotten you? Every time I see Regina or any of the old crowd I ask about you."[102] Regina remained lifelong friends with Ethel, who credited Regina as being the pivotal person that held the salon together. She recalled, "Regina was our life saver. She was . . . very special. . . . She loved to have people around her, she was quite a social individual."[103]

4. Marriage

Regina, like many young women in New York City, had a dating life that was complicated, diverse, and mysterious. She had more than one fiancé, a long distance relationship, a possible affair with a Jewish writer, and a secret lover—the author of a "Dear Reggie" letter who may have been the one she truly loved but her family disapproved of the liaison.

Back at 580 St. Nicholas Avenue the trio invited their boyfriends to dinner. Regina knew how to set "the most wonderful table"—a skill she probably learned from her mother who also most likely painted the china that was used for the dinner. Regina spread a beautiful tablecloth, the "proper silver" and candles on the table. Regina knew how to make "the most delicious salads" but not all the courses that followed. According to Ethel Nance, Regina once ordered, "now Ethel you can fry the chicken." Ethel replied, "fry the chicken, I don't know how to fry chicken." Regina said, "I have never fried chicken." "Here we were in the kitchen," Ethel recalled, "wondering what we were going to do about the main item on the menu. We got together and somehow or other we did what we thought should be done, but the horrors of that meal. We sat there afraid to try it ourselves and waiting for the guests to take the first bite."[1]

In *Nigger Heaven*, Carl Van Vechten's fictional Regina and Ethel have the following exchange: Mary suggests that she cook for her date. Olive declares, "Say, Mary, don't scare the man away. You prepare your first meal for him after you're married. It will be too late for him to leave you then."[2]

The name of Regina's boyfriend who was invited to the fried chicken dinner is unknown, but during this time she would visit another man in another state and write letters that could be characterized as love letters to a third man. In 1924, Regina went to Normal, Illinois, on vacation to look after her ill mother. During this time, Regina wrote at least two letters to her friend, Joseph Freeman, suggesting a possible romance. In a handwritten undated letter composed on a Wednesday, Regina wished that Joseph was with her in Normal so that they could walk "under the elms" while the sun was setting and fireflies could light their way.[3] In an another undated handwritten letter composed on a Tuesday, Regina wrote, "Hope some evening when I return you will come up when there is not a party, and talk with me about your books, your work, interests, Etc."[4] Regina ended the Wednesday letter by telling Freeman, "I return to Chicago from here and then to Cleveland, Ohio." She would obviously visit her father in Chicago, but she does not mention her plans for Cleveland. An item in the *Chicago Defender*'s "The Buckeye State" section, Cleveland Society News (which Joseph most likely did not read), mentioned that a guest of honor, Miss Regina Anderson of New York, was visiting Mr. and Mrs. E. J. Lucas in Salem, Ohio. The item revealed that at a luncheon, "A. St. George Richardson, fiancé of Miss Anderson, of course was also a guest."[5] So Regina was engaged when she was writing letters to Joseph. Richardson would not become her husband.

Bermuda-born Arthur St. George Richardson was a bank cashier and former educator—president of Wilberforce Institute in Chatham, Ontario. He was born in 1863 and came to the United States in 1887. He became president of Morris Brown College in Atlanta, Georgia, the following year and presided there until 1898. However, this would make Richardson sixty-one at the time of the engagement when Regina was twenty-three! A biographical sketch of the elder Richardson in the 1915 publication *Who's Who of the Colored Race* indicated that he had two sons—one a namesake who was Regina's fiancé.[6] Decades later, Regina's niece Lorelei speculated that Richardson was the love of her life; her parents disapproved of him because he was so dark, although pictures of his father do not reveal a dark-skinned man but a man with definite African American features. Perhaps her parents also disapproved of the West Indian background of his parents.

There is an unusual inclusion of a letter in Regina's papers from an unknown paramour. Either a second page is missing or the author did not sign the missive because she would know who sent it. Although there are possible hints about the identity of the writer, which include the schools he attended, the author remains unknown. Maybe the author was Richardson, but which schools, if any, he attended have not been identified. The letter is dated September 24th in the morning and the author addresses Regina as "Dear Reggie":

> It is very late or rather early, but this is the only time I seem to have available to write to you. Today I went up to Ohio State to take my books and some other items. The trip was tiring, so when I got back home I took a two hour and a half nap. That's the reason I feel I should be capable of writing you an intelligible letter. I'll now set about to prove how wrong that last sentence is. I noticed in your letter to me that you did not comment on what I had said in the letter to you and the same that I had reiterated over the phone, the effect of separation on our relationship, on a workable one. There are really three answers that your silence on the matter conveys: that you completely agree; that you completely disagree; or that you deemed discussion of the matter unnecessary. I tend now to agree with the last possibility and hope that you have chosen it too. I wish no longer to push anything, especially not you. I want us to be whatever we can to one another without calling-up any bugaboos to pressure that which we do share together. Enough said on this. School officially begins for me this coming Monday. I'm going back to State this Friday though to get organized and oriented into the campus life. My intention is not to make State another Syracuse for me. Don't misunderstand me: I liked and do love Syracuse as my first alma mater, but my staying there was seemingly [more] distructive [sic] than beneficial. Another reason for my transferring to State is that my accume will begin with the first marks I receive at the end of the Fall quarter. And a 4.0 will be my goal. I've decided to make something of myself, to find myself just as you seem to have been able to find yourself. With a high accume I'll have a much better chance of getting into the med school I desire to attend (no I haven't picked it out as yet). Enclosed is an article from the Saturday Review on one of existentualism's [sic] greatest exponents, Sartre. It is sort of disheartening to find out that a man, any man who bases his entire life on and for the promotion of a particular philosophy would publically [sic] denounce himself to be a hypocrite. But as D. H. Lawrence says, "Trust not the author, but the author's words."[7]

Despite having this mysterious admirer, Regina continued her correspondence with Freeman. In a letter on NYPL stationary Regina wrote to Freeman about a proposed meeting: "Rather unpardonably careless of me to have forgotten that I am working here until nine, Wednesday night. So may I ask you to come Monday night, at seven, instead. If that is not convenient Thursday will be quite alright. However if I do not hear from you to the contrary may I expect you Monday?"[8] Then, in 1925, also on work stationary she adds a handwritten note to the typed letter inviting him to speak at the North Harlem Community Forum: "Would you call Saturday or Monday night after 10 (P.M.) Audobon 10099 Apt. 5K?" A rather late night visit but perhaps not that unusual. In *Nig-*

ger Heaven, Mary Love entertained a boyfriend rather late at night: "The bell did not ring again till ten-thirty. Mary ran to answer it."[9]

*   *   *

A little over a year after inviting Freeman to her apartment, Regina married another man—Bill Andrews. Regina recalled, "I had met Bill Andrews at a dance. Got to know him. He was in law school at the time and we found that we had many mutual friends including Jessie Fauset who was a friend of mine."[10] Bill was a more suitable candidate than Richardson, who was too dark and "exotic" because of his West Indian heritage, or Freeman, who was too white, Jewish, and Communist. Bill was fair, tall, and handsome; librarian Jean Blackwell Hutson recalled that Regina was "quite the envy of the women of that day."[11] Bill was enrolled in law school at Columbia (where Regina would later attend), had graduated from a Black university, like Regina, and came from a family similar in background. Both of their fathers were named William and pulled themselves up by their bootstraps to rise to a comfortable upper-middle-class existence as lawyers, although lacking the old-money connections. They both shared an interest in acting and moved in the same social circles.

Bill and Regina were among a group of people invited to an exclusive party in 1923 in Green Lake, New York, hosted by Lillian Turner Alexander and her husband Dr. Ernest Alexander, a prominent physician at Harlem Hospital. The Alexanders were very important people who also lived in the Sugar Hill section of Harlem, although "they could have lived anywhere they wanted in New York." Lillian Turner Alexander was from St. Paul, Minnesota, and looked out for Regina's roommate, Ethel, as a fellow Minnesotan. Lillian Alexander made it her "duty to be sure that little Ethel from Duluth came to no harm." Lillian already knew Regina from the library and "so when she learned that I was living with Regina, she said, 'oh well now I know that you're all right.'" The Alexanders hosted an annual picnic, and Ethel recalled, "[I]f you were invited to the Alexanders' annual picnic, you were in." Further, she stated, "[I]f you were invited to the Alexanders' picnic as I was informed, during the *first year* you were in New York, you were really *in*."[12] So Bill and Regina were both *in*.

Bill was born on June 11, 1898, in Sumter, South Carolina. The city of Sumter (pronounced as if there was a p after the m) is also the county seat of Sumter County. The twenty-six-square-mile city, situated in the middle of the state, is located approximately forty-four miles from the capital, Columbia. Bill was the older of two sons born to William Trent Andrews Sr. (who signed his letters as W. T.) and Anna Lee Andrews. A few years later, his brother Norman Perry, known as "Perry," joined him. He received his bachelor's degree in 1921 from Howard University, an institution that his father attended for his law degree. After graduation, Bill taught at Pennsylvania Avenue High School in Baltimore before moving to New York City to attend law school at Columbia University.

Bill's father, W. T., was born on March 25, 1864, in Sumter, South Carolina. He began working at the age of thirteen when he was put in charge of his father's small grocery store. Interestingly, Regina's own father briefly owned a grocery store in Chicago in 1890.[13] The 1880 Census recorded sixteen-year-old W. T.'s occupation as a huckster—"[o]ne who sells wares or provisions in the street; a peddler or hawker."[14]

A few years later, on June 14, 1885, twenty-one-year-old W. T. became a cadet at West Point. He left less than a year later on January 21, 1886, due to the poor treatment of Negro students.[15] Regrouping, he attended Fisk University in 1886 and then enrolled in Howard University Law School, graduating in 1892. W. T. was the only African American listed among those who passed the bar in South Carolina in 1894. He married Anna in 1896 and, two years later, Regina's future husband, William Trent Andrews Jr., was born.

Andrews Sr. worked variously as a lawyer, insurance agent, businessman, realtor, newspaper editor, journalist, Methodist Reformer, and political figure. By 1915, he owned "60 houses, 4 brick business buildings and part interest in 9 store buildings," and was considered "[t]he largest Negro tax payer in the city" of Sumter.[16] He was the editor and publisher of a weekly newspaper, the *Defender*, in Sumter and later started another paper in 1917, the *Herald*, after moving to Baltimore, Maryland.

*   *   *

Like her mother, Regina married an attorney officially named William. Initially they planned to wed at a local church, St. Philips Church on 134th Street, the venue of choice among Harlem's black elite. This church was attended by "the wealthiest African-American congregation in New York. The majority of its members were light-skinned African Americans."[17] Regina recalled, referring to novelist Fauset, "when I announced that I was to get married Jessie and her sister were hoping I would have it (the wedding) in their home"[18] located in the apartment building at 1945 Seventh Avenue between 117th and 118th Streets in Harlem. Fauset also hosted a luncheon for the couple before the wedding, and Gladys Hurst hosted a prewedding breakfast for the wedding party at Craig's Restaurant on the day of the ceremony.

At the time of the wedding, Bill also lived at 1945 Seventh Avenue, which would become the newlyweds' first home. Regina lived at 260 West 139th Street. Bill was twenty-seven and Regina was twenty-five, and Bill's occupation was listed as "law clerk." There was no space on the bride's portion of the marriage certificate to indicate her occupation. They were both listed as colored, and their witnesses were Jessie Fauset and Hubert Delany.[19]

The wedding was reported in all of the major African American newspapers. The *Chicago Defender* called the ceremony "[o]ne of the leading social events of the season." The wedding was on Saturday, April 10, 1926, at five P.M. and attended by "[a] small group of relatives and intimate friends."[20] Reverend Shelton Hale Bishop from St. Philips officiated. Oddly, Regina's father did not attend the wedding. There may have been bad blood between her parents fifteen years after their divorce. It must have been a difficult day for Regina, who was close to her father, because he was not there to walk her down the aisle. Perhaps he had an important court case. Nevertheless, other family members were present, including Regina's mother, who gave her away. Bill's father escorted her mother in the processional. Bill's younger brother Perry served as best man. Bertha McNeil and poet Clarissa Scott, both from Washington, served as bridesmaids along with Crystal Byrd and Mrs. Lyle Carter from New York City. Ushers included Dr. Charles B. Howard from Philadelphia, F. D. Johnson, and Edwin Coates from New York City. Charles S. Johnson from *Opportunity* was the ring bearer. Regina's gown was "white satin trimmed with the same pearls that had adorned her mother's wedding dress," and, as something borrowed, "a handkerchief that her mother carried on her wedding day."[21]

The reception was located in the same building but in the apartment of the newlyweds: "The elite of New York passed down the reception line and inspected the many handsome presents which were on display."[22] After the reception the newlyweds honeymooned in Atlantic City, New Jersey. Regina's change in status was duly noted in the "New York Society" column in the *Pittsburgh Courier*. Columnist Mrs. H. Binga Dismond announced, "Petite Miss Regina Anderson henceforth and forever more will be petite Mrs. Regina Andrews, wife of Attorney William Andrews and has been transferred from the social register of Harlem's misses to the section headed, Young Society Matrons." Regina's new husband was described as "young Bill Andrews belonging to the illustrious Andrewses of Baltimore."[23]

It was ironic that Regina's wedding was a low-key affair compared to her parents' elaborate celebration—wedding in one state, reception in another, and guest list of six hundred. Regina's marriage would long outlast that of her parents.

* * *

At the time of her wedding, Regina was no longer working at the 135th Street Branch. She wrote to her friend, writer Joseph Freeman, saying, "Moving and getting settled in a new home, have kept me rather busy . . . [a]lso having been recently transferred to another Library on East Houston Street, I find myself spending quite a bit of time on the subways."[24] Regina was now working at the Hamilton Fish Park Branch. Freeman noted that Eric (most likely a reference to Eric Walrond, a West Indian writer) told him that Regina had moved several weeks ago. He noted, "From the telephone number in your letter it looks like a long, long trip for you to the East Side every day: enough to drive even the wisest to cross-word puzzles."[25] Like other NYPL branches, this branch suffered from a lack of funds to purchase books. Children attending the local P.S. (public school) 188 put on a play and donated the proceeds, $66.75, to the Children's Department at the Hamilton Fish Branch for the purchase of books.[26] Regina would remain at this branch for just two months before being transferred to the Woodstock Branch in the Bronx. She would be their first African American librarian. Ernestine Rose, the Branch Librarian at the 135th Street Library, believed "that a mixed staff renders more valuable service to the community and the general public."[27] Rose felt that other branches of the NYPL had begun to follow suit after her branch and cited Regina's transfer to the Woodstock Branch as an example of staff integration.

On October 1, 1927, Regina was appointed to the position of assistant in school work at the Woodstock Branch located in the Bronx at 761 East 160th Street. Although she was promoted, she probably did not receive a large pay increase if she received any at all. The NYPL librarians had not had any raises in five years and, since there was not a pension plan, librarians were not quick to retire.[28] At this branch, Regina worked under the Branch Librarian Augusta Markowitz. Regina's transfer "came in recognition of her increased efficiency" and unlike her work in Harlem, at this branch "all of her work is done among white students."[29] The now landmark building was the "three-story" Woodstock Branch library, a "palazzo-style" structure opened in 1914 "designed by McKim, Mead & White." The building "has a classically inspired façade clad in rusticated limestone and features an offset entrance, carved stone ornament, and tall, arched windows on the first floor and a frieze topped by a simple limestone cornice."[30] This section of the Bronx was home to a Hungarian community, and earlier Markowitz had traveled to Hungary during the summer to purchase new Hungarian titles for this branch and two other NYPL branches that served this group of immigrants.[31] This branch also offered English language classes for its foreign-born patrons.[32] All of the library branches reported the number of foreign language books in their collections in their annual reports sent to the director. They also noted increases and decreases in particular languages, which provided information about the makeup of various neighborhoods. The branches made efforts to honor their patrons' heritage by providing books in their native tongues; one example would be an exhibit of Hungarian industrial art at the Woodstock Branch.[33]

The library did not neglect its English-speaking patrons. Markowitz requested $500 to purchase more books after discovering one day, while shelving books when the regular page was absent, that the collection was lacking in the classics. She was horrified to find that the collection contained no works by Austen, Balzac, Dumas, Doyle, or London, and no copies of *Don Quixote, Oliver Twist, Tale of Two Cities,* or *Vanity Fair.*[34] The branch also hosted several meetings, including several sponsored by the Board of Education; Bronx Women's Federation for Social Service; City History Club; Bronx Continuation School (five book talks); Council of Jewish Women; Girl Scouts of the Bronx Troops 4, 21, and 38; Social Problems Graduate Club; Woodstock Literary Club; Hebrew Orphan Asylum-Foster Mothers, Hebrew Sheltering and Immigrant Aid Society-Citizenship class; and the Poetry Club of Junior High School, P.S. 51.

Regina gave an interview to the *Pittsburgh Courier* about her new position integrating a library branch. She shared her philosophy about librarianship as a career for African American women: "Library work is a difficult field, requiring a great deal of study and training. . . . The chances for colored girls, of course, are not the best, but I do believe that if they meet the requirements they will receive appointments to important posts the same as others."[35] Like teaching, librarianship was considered an acceptable profession for middle-class African American women.

After her wedding, Regina enrolled in Columbia University's School of Library Service Extension program between 1926 and 1928. Her enrollment immediately after her wedding indicated that neither Regina nor Bill planned to start a family right away and may have practiced birth control (indicated by Regina's support of a speech by Margaret Sanger). Now Bill was ready to begin practicing law, and the Andrewses were able to afford to enroll Regina at Columbia, which was conveniently located in the Morningside Heights section of New York City next to Harlem where Regina lived. Had Regina been single, she would not have been allowed to live on campus. Librarian Dorothy Porter Wesley, who attended the program after Regina, said, "I couldn't get a room in the dormitory. I couldn't live in the dormitory. I had to live on Riverside Drive because of my color."[36]

Columbia University's School of Library Service was originally called the School of Library Economy when it began in 1887 under the direction of Melvil Dewey, then the librarian of Columbia College and the creator of the Dewey Decimal Classification System.[37] The School moved to Albany two years later when Dewey became the director of the State Library until the School returned to Columbia University in 1926 under the direction of Dr. Charles C. Williamson. The American Library Association standards mandated that library schools should be associated with degree-granting institutions. The new edition of the School was consolidated with the New York Public Library's own Library School. The resources of both schools, including faculty and a $25,000-a-year grant from the Carnegie Corporation to the NYPL Library School, were combined to form the new School of Library Service at Columbia.

Regina was part of the first wave of students to enroll in the new edition of Columbia University's School of Library Service. Although various biographical encyclopedias state that she completed a library degree from Columbia University, her transcripts indicate that she took only a few courses.[38]

Regina was enrolled in the University Extension program and not the master's degree-granting program.[39] She is listed as Regina Mildred Andrews of 405 Edgecombe Ave. The University Extension program was for candidates with at least one year of college education who demonstrated that they possessed "the requisite personal qualifications for library work" demonstrated by currently working in a library. The final requirement was a "reasonable facility in typewriting."[40] After completing an admissions application the candidate also had to provide official transcripts for the undergraduate institution and a certificate from a doctor that assured the applicant was in good health.[41]

Dr. Melvil Dewey addressed the audience at the opening exercises of the School of Library Service. Perhaps Regina attended. Unfortunately, his speech was not preserved because "he had not prepared a written speech and he spoke too rapidly for the stenographer to get more than a few fragments."[42]

During the fall 1926 term, Regina took Library Service 107—the first part of the Cataloguing and Subject Headings sequence. During spring 1927, she took Library Service 108, the second part of the sequence, and she completed Library Service 105—Reference Service—during fall 1927. The courses were offered at night so that employed librarians could attend after working hours. Library Service 107 and 108 were offered on Tuesday and Wednesday nights from 7–9:30 P.M., which made for a long day for Regina.

In his first annual report to the president of Columbia University, Director Williamson summarized the first year of the new School of Library Service. He noted that students enrolled in the Extension program, like Regina, "represented a high level of ability and more experience on the average than the graduate students."[43] In his second annual report, Director Williamson stated that no one had completed the certificate yet because most of the students enrolled in the Extension program worked full time and could only enroll in a few courses at a time. He stated, "Many students who take these courses desire merely to get more information or training in special subjects and do not plan to complete the work for the certificate."[44] Regina was among these students. She did not enroll in any more courses after the fall 1927 term.

*   *   *

During this time, Bill passed the New York State bar.[45] Regina's mother wrote Bill a letter of "Hearty congratulations!" She said, "I am sure you deserve all the flowers you get, of course I have thot [*sic*] of nothing but success for you for my daily prayer has been that God would crown your efforts with success." She continued by noting that both he and Regina were surely happy about this outcome. In reference to Bill's late mother, she said, "I am sure the good spirit of your mother has hovered near to encourage you and you have thot [*sic*] often how happy she would be were she here to give you a hearty kiss and press you to heart, for these are the blessings that come to a mother when she sees her children pushing on and mounting the ladder to fame, in as much as she is not here in person I will take her place." She reminds him, "Now you can have little cards printed and use the little silver case which I gave you five years ago." This last statement reveals that Regina knew Bill from the time of her arrival in Harlem and that her mother felt close enough to Bill to give him an expensive gift. However, Regina was engaged to someone else during some of this time period. Her mother mentioned, in her letter to Bill, that she was on her way to spend several months in Normal, Illinois, because there were ten college girls living at 405 North Fell Avenue. She signed off as "Mother" but not before mentioning that she had "written Regina several letters but she doesn't seem to be able to answer any of them."[46]

Bill opened a private practice first at 2313 Seventh Avenue and later relocated in 1929 to 200 West 135th Street.[47] He also worked part-time as a special counsel to the NAACP. He was a member of the National Bar Association (NBA) and the NYC Bar Association.[48] One of Bill's first private practice cases to be reported in the African American press involved a woman who received $500 after being assaulted by a store proprietor.[49] Later, Bill was somewhat less successful when he defended a man charged with first degree murder who was convicted of manslaughter in the first degree. Bill argued on his behalf for self-defense during a poolroom brawl.[50] For his work with the NAACP, Bill fought causes ranging from discrimination to a case involving a university student who was shot in the back by a police officer.[51] In 1931, Bill represented cast members of the play *Green Pastures* who accused a police officer of "abusing and insulting them as they were getting in a taxicab" after a performance.[52] The police officer later confessed his guilt and was fined a day's pay.[53]

During their third year of marriage, Bill wrote several love letters to Regina over a two-week period in July 1928 when Regina was visiting family in Illinois. Using stationary from his law office, Bill addressed Regina variously as "Sweetheart," "Dearest," "Dearest little girl," "Dearest girl," and "Dear Bunch." He asked her, "You are a bunch aren't you? And you are dear, so you are a 'dear bunch.'"

When Regina was out of town Bill ate dinner of "salad, rice, greens, lettuce and tomato salad and watermelon" at the African American YMCA Branch in Harlem.[54] Afterward, he headed back to his office at 2313 Seventh Avenue before eventually heading home. He told Regina:

> I thought of you all the way from the station to Harlem and while eating. But it was when I turned the key in the lock, pulled the cord to the hall light, that I wanted to catch that train and either go with you or bring you back. Here I was at our home, and you were not here, but worst yet, you would not be here at all tonight or for many nights. It was unreal, not the home I had for so longed.

Bill mentioned the noise of firecrackers—it was the Fourth of July—and continued his lament:

> My other letters will not be telling you how I feel without you for I shall not break the joy of this trip for you for a moment—only in this the first will I allow myself to say, I miss you so much that I want you here or I want to be where you are.

He ended the letter with "May the peace of Allah abide with you. Yours, and your husband, Bill." Then a P S noting that her telegram arrived as he finished writing that letter. His last line was "Good night dearest, Bill."[55]

Bill chided her in his next letter, where he stated, "I did not write you last night because I was beginning to think that you had completely neglected me. So I was getting angry and had resolved to punish you by not writing you." But after receiving a missive from Regina he decided to write that letter. Regina wrote that she had been ill but still enjoyed a visit with her father and her brother Maurice. A friend of theirs, Sally, invited Bill to dinner. He noted, "It will be my 1st meal at a home since you have been gone."[56] He ended by passing on a greeting to Regina's mother. While Regina was gone Bill kept himself occupied with his work for both his private practice and the NAACP and by visiting friends. He was stood up for an engagement to play tennis but enjoyed chatting at dinner with their friends Ern and Sally. He mentioned eating watermelon with friends too—a recurring theme. Bill assured Regina,

"Everybody misses you so." The previous night he spoke with Regina and her mother by phone and noted that he could hear the excitement of Regina's visit in her mother's voice. He asked Regina in the letter, "What have you talked about—me! Told her about my good traits and short comings which have been discovered in two years? Are they any of the latter?"[57]

Once again, Bill went by their friend Sally's "to play some bridge and lo,—there were others—Bennie and Anne, Margaret Smith-Douglass, two girls from Washington Misses Simmons and Harris; we played until 12, ate a whole watermelon—One girl did not eat it, so each of us had an eighth(!)." Later, "at 12:30 or 12:45—we all—but the two Washington girls," got into "Ern and Margaret's cars and went for a long ride. Got home 1:30 or 1:45 dead asleep on my feet. It was all so delightful though. It was a hot night too." Bill lamented, "I had no one to hug. It would have been so great if you had been there in Ern's car with me." He asked Regina, "Have you been telling Mother how you miss me and wish I were along. Well, why not?" He related that, on behalf of the NAACP, he "got a girl out of jail who was held charged with larceny." He said he would not be attending a reception for summer students at the 135th Street Branch that evening, stating, "I don't recall that we were urged to be present."[58]

Bill wrote the last letter on Friday the 13th and observed, "This is the day which is suppose to be so terrible and always a jinx but it brought me good luck. When I came home at about 11 o'clock I found your second letter awaiting me. I was so happy. Of course I am not going to ask you to come home. But I do want you with me." He reports that he may have to go to Scranton, Pennsylvania, the following Sunday and Monday to give two speeches on behalf of the NAACP. Bill ended the note with an ambiguous message: "Wouldn't it be wonderful if we could and did have one of the dears you wanted in your letter in the coming year. Regina, how happy we would be." Was he referring to having a child? They would eventually raise a child but most likely not in the way they initially expected. He ended the letter by stating, "I'll send you a small check on Tuesday."[59]

* * *

During the early years of her marriage, Regina was involved with the local Rho chapter of Delta Sigma Theta, an African American sorority, and served as the president. The organization was founded in 1913 at Howard University. Famous past and present members of the sorority include Lena Horne, Mary McLeod Bethune, Mary Church Terrell, Barbara Jordan, Judith Jamison, Wilma Rudolph, and Nikki Giovanni, among others.[60] Bill was a member of an African American fraternity, Alpha Phi Alpha. The Andrewses attended a formal hosted by the fraternity.[61]

Regina appeared a few times in the *New York Amsterdam News* "With the Sororities" column. In 1927, her chapter sponsored a trip to Indian Point, New York. The blurb does not mention what they did there, but it noted that Regina's husband was one of the guests along with a few other men.[62] In 1929, Regina hosted a Sunday afternoon tea in her home at 405 Edgecombe Avenue.[63] Finally, in 1934, the 135th Street Branch hosted a program for the Deltas for junior and senior high school students to learn about various career options. Regina did not speak about library careers—Dorothy Robinson did. Regina spoke about career options in the dramatic arts—no doubt because of her experiences with the little theater movement.[64]

5. The Harlem Experimental Theatre

Regina's participation in the little theater movement began with her involvement with the theater company founded by her friend W. E. B. Du Bois. Sometime during 1924, Du Bois contacted Supervising Librarian Ernestine Rose and asked for permission to use the basement of the 135th Street Branch for a theater group, named the CRIGWA Players.[1] CRIGWA stood for Crisis Guild of Writers and Artists named after the *Crisis* journal. Later the group's name was changed to the KRIGWA Players. Du Bois wanted to use the basement stage to produce "three or four plays in 1926 and from four to six plays in 1927." Both Regina and her husband Bill were members of the KRIGWA Players board.

Du Bois's often-quoted philosophy about the KRIGWA was the following:

> [T]he plays of a Negro theatre must be: 1. About us. That is, they must have plots which reveal Negro life as it is. 2. By us. That is, they must be written by Negro authors who understand from birth and continued association just what it means to be a Negro today. 3. For us. That is, the theatre must cater primarily to Negro audiences and be supported and sustained by their entertainment and approval. 4. Near us. The theatre must be in a Negro neighborhood near the mass of ordinary Negro people.[2]

The creation of the KRIGWA Players and other little theaters throughout the nation was a response to plays that portrayed African Americans in a negative light as ignorant, shuffling, inarticulate caricatures. To add insult to injury, African American characters were often portrayed by white actors in blackface.

Regina's husband Bill acted in plays staged by the KRIGWA Players. He played Sam in performances of *The Broken Banjo* in May 1926. Six years later, noted thespian Rose McClendon directed him in a Broadway play about a lynching, *Never No More*. The *New York Amsterdam News* review stated that he was "surprisingly excellent as Joe."[3] McClendon would later become involved in Regina's theater company. Several months later, Bill performed in the production of the play *Bloodstream* about escaped convicts in a Times Square theater. The reviewer didn't think much of the writing but said, "The defects of the drama, however, are supplemented by the unusually fine acting of a superior cast. . . . William Andrews and Ernest Whitman turn in memorable performances."[4] Regina would later act on the stage too.

The relationship between Du Bois's KRIGWA Players and the 135th Street Branch ended on a sour note. In a series of increasingly contentious notes from Du Bois to librarian Ernestine Rose and, in her absence, to her assistant Eliza Buckner Marquess, Du Bois expressed unhappiness with keeping the KRIGWA players housed in the library branch. Earlier, in January 1927, Du Bois asked Rose to grant a theater group, the Sekondi Players, permission to rehearse in the basement theater in anticipation of their subsequent performances at the 135th Street Branch. Later Du Bois declared, "I feel strongly concerning the matter and if the Sekondi Players appear in the library basement I should feel that I would have to withdraw my co-operation. They are not at all up to our standard."[5] It is unclear what the nature of the dispute was between Du Bois about the Sekondi Players or what he meant by "our standard." Perhaps Du Bois felt that the Sekondi Players's performances were not the propaganda-type plays that he favored. Eventually, Du Bois posted an ad in the *New York Amsterdam News*, noting the end of the partnership between KRIGWA and the 135th Street Branch. Rose reluctantly agreed to the end of the relationship.[6] There also were disputes about what to do with the profits from the performances. Du Bois wanted to put the funds back into KRIGWA productions, but actors, playwrights, and other behind-the-scenes players wanted to be financially rewarded for their contributions.

It is unknown whether Regina had knowledge of this situation, and if so, what her position was on the issues. She would have had divided loyalties to her employer and friend, Du Bois. After the demise of the KRIGWA Players, several people, including Regina and actors Dorothy Peterson and Harold Jackman, met in the basement of the 135th Street Branch and discussed forming a theater group loosely modeled on KRIGWA. Peterson was a teacher, and Jackman was an actor and teacher who graduated from New York University and received a master's degree from Columbia University.

Regina recalled: "We began to talk about wanting to write and produce our own dramas. Plays and revues of black people were on downtown stages, but few were presented in Harlem where the black playwright's audience lived.

We had few plays to work with and almost none of recent date."[7] According to their brochure: "The Harlem Experimental Theatre offers opportunities for young Negro Playwrights and Actors who wish to aid in the Negro's Contribution to Art in America. We welcome original plays for consideration and new talent as we plan to emphasize Negro Drama." Regina served as the executive director of the theater company, and the advisory board, which Regina called, "a wonderful board of advisors, all extremely cooperative,"[8] included W. E. B. Du Bois (despite the earlier dispute with the KRIGWA Players); his "rival" Alain Locke; Jessie Fauset; Rose McClendon, an accomplished Broadway actress and director; and Mary White Ovington, a white woman who was one of the founders of the National Association for the Advancement of Colored People (NAACP). Fauset was later put in charge of selecting plays from the HET submissions. Aaron Douglas created posters and playbills, including the logo for the Harlem Experimental Theatre.[9]

In addition to the board of advisors, the HET received financial support and encouragement from "financially secure Harlemites and a few downtowners," perhaps code words for African Americans and white people, respectively.[10]

Although the HET was allegedly modeled after Du Bois's KRIGWA Players, it did not follow Du Bois's manifesto to produce plays by and about African American people. Regina explained that the HET decided: "In the beginning . . . we would not limit ourselves to Negro plays until we could produce our own. So, our first production was 'The Duchess Says Her Prayers' by Mary Cass Canfield and 'The No 'Count Boy' by Paul Green."[11] Green's play *In Abraham's Bosom* won the 1927 Pulitzer Prize, and he was also awarded a Guggenheim Fellowship. Green was considered to be "[o]ne of the most visible white writers and playwrights of the Harlem Renaissance era and author of plays hailed for their representations of African American life and identity."[12] Scholar Adrienne Macki suggested that Regina's own mixed-race background may have influenced the HET's philosophy of offering plays by both white and African American playwrights. Macki also suggested that perhaps they relied on plays by white playwrights due to the lack of available plays by African American playwrights.[13] However, it appears that the HET board members made a conscious effort not to limit their productions by race while at the same time they assisted budding African American playwrights to put their work on the stage. The HET later produced plays by African American playwrights, including two of Regina's. She elaborated on the philosophy behind the HET, stating that "we have not limited ourselves to the production of Negro plays feeling that our people are just as capable of depicting the spontaneity, tragedy, and happiness of life as we see it and feel it—Negro life as we live it." The plans for the HET included: "First: To establish a permanent Little Theatre in Harlem. Second: To make a definite contribution to Negro Drama and Literature by encouraging the writing of plays and producing them. Third: To train and develop talent for the stage."[14]

In a 1934 radio speech, "The Community Theater: A Part of the Life of the People," Regina said:

> We have given special attention to the production of original unpublished plays by Negroes. After four years of work with our theater, I feel that our greatest contribution to the cultural achievement of the community will be in this pro-duction of original plays. . . . We must develop our Negro drama to include the problem of the Negro worker and the present day Negro social drama theme. At present, these themes are unexploited.[15]

The theater group was initially located in the 135th Street Branch before moving to St. Philip's Church Parish House. This change of venue was a turning point for the HET because one of the most accomplished Broadway theater members, Rose McClendon, became a director for the HET. She brought professional experience and encouraged them to produce original material.[16] Born in 1884 in Greenville, South Carolina, she moved to New York City after 1900. McClendon was awarded a scholarship to attend the American Academy of Dramatic Arts and performed in numerous plays, in-cluding one costarring Paul Robeson. She formed the Negro People's Theater in Harlem with Dick Campbell. McClendon also worked with white director John Houseman on the Black Unit of the Federal Theater Project.

Like many theater groups in the Little Theater Movement, the playwrights, directors, actors, costume designers, and lighting crews were self-taught be-cause of the lack of educational opportunities for African Americans at that time. One goal of the HET was to create a school to train African Americans interested in theater careers. For example, the HET conducted a playwrit-ing class cotaught by a Broadway playwright, Pierre Loving. Paul Glick, the former director of the Little Theatre in San Antonio, Texas, taught another course. Both Regina and Robert Dorsey took Loving's class and later had their respective plays, *Underground* and *Waxen Lily*, performed by the HET.[17]

The HET continued to receive praise from theater professionals when a Broadway star attended one of their productions and gave parts to two HET actresses, including Dorothy Peterson. Regina replaced Peterson's role in the HET production.

In her radio speech, Regina declared:

> It can be truly said that the community theater is an important factor in the educational, social, and recreational life of the people. It supplies an outlet for self-expression which is inherent in all of us. It provides a stimulant or an

incentive to personality improvement. In many cases the little theater has been the instrument for unearthing real talent. Perhaps one of the most productive agencies in this regard has been our own little theater group, The Harlem Experimental Theatre. The story of the struggles and achievements of this group is representative of similar groups in other communities. The need it has filled in a Negro community like Harlem cannot be estimated.[18]

Macki argued that the HET represented differences in the "existing class hierarchies," between Harlem's African American communities. She stated that "the group's subscription list suggests a distinctly class-based patronage, drawing from Harlem's educated upper- and middle-class blacks, which directly paralleled the group's administrative management under Andrews, Jackman, and Dorothy Peterson."[19] Macki concluded that "HET's representation of race was often contradictory and class-based, which potentially perpetuated hierarchical power relations even as it intended to dispel the larger problems of racial marginalization."[20]

Regina and her husband were among the more fortunate people of any race during the Depression. On June, 1, 1930, a year after the start of the Great Depression in 1929, Regina was transferred to the now defunct Rivington Street Branch of NYPL and promoted from Grade 2 to Grade 3 (assistant branch librarian). That year's Census would record 195 African Americans listing the occupation of librarian.[21] Regina was still among a small number of African Americans in the profession. Due to her promotion, Regina received a $10 a month salary increase to $165, or $1,980 a year.[22]

The Rivington Street Branch had the distinction of having NYPL's first open-air rooftop garden opened in 1905:

> The reference department of the library was on the third floor next to the roof and was unbearably hot. So it occurred to the authorities to try the experiment of letting the people there take the books they were using on to the roof. There was no doubt of the success of the plan, for in that first trial Summer nearly 7,500 readers climbed the extra flight of stairs to enjoy the forty-four-square[-foot] "roof garden."[23]

The rooftop gardens had awnings over the tables in case of rain and electric lights to permit patrons to read after sundown. Besides the rooftop garden, this branch hosted several meetings of local organizations, including the Italian Girls' Club, semimonthly meetings of the Yiddish Mother's Club, lectures "New York and Its Environs" and "Vocational Guidance," readings from the works of Jewish authors, and a reading from his own work by Paul Stein, Jewish author and dramatist. Regina would remain at this branch until 1936 working for Branch Librarian Elizabeth Kamenetzky.

Around this time, her husband, Bill, was employed as special legal counsel for the NAACP from 1927–1932. His salary is unknown, but the average annual salary was around $1,000.[24] Regina made almost twice that amount on her salary alone. After being let go by the NAACP due to financial constraints, Bill became an assemblyman from 1935–1948, representing Harlem with his focus on the economic, educational, and health concerns experienced by his constituency. Neither Regina nor Bill was unaware of the concerns of the African Americans living in Harlem. While most African Americans in her community were struggling to make a living, Regina was involved in extracurricular activities related to the HET. Theater critic Theophilus Lewis acerbically noted in his newspaper column: "The membership of the Harlem Experimental Theatre consists of an ideal working personnel for a little theatre—the wives of well fixed business and professional men."[25] This was not entirely fair to people like Regina, who was both educated and employed.

There is no indication about what the NYPL administration thought of Regina's HET work. At some level there may have initially been tacit approval, which allowed the HET to begin by using the basement of the 135th Street Branch. No reason was given for the theater company's subsequent moves to St. Philip's Episcopal Church and the YMCA.

Nevertheless, despite the continuing social and economic concerns of many of Harlem's African Americans during the Depression, the HET continued putting on performances for the usual price of fifty cents for three one-act plays—the equivalent of about $7.67 in current terms. Theater critics from several African American newspapers, the *Chicago Defender*, the *New York Age*, and the *New York Amsterdam News*, reviewed the performances of the HET, including Regina's.

A reviewer critiqued Regina's performance in *A Sunny Morning* as "a charming short play of Spanish life," by the Quintero Brothers from the Andalusia region of Spain. The reviewer stated that "[s]pecial credit is due both Mrs. Andrews and Mr. [Edler G.] Hawkins for their excellent interpretation of their parts as old people."[26] Another reviewer, Brenda Ray Moryck said, "Andrews, as the little old Spanish grand dame, was superb. Her natural beauty, delicate and fragile, combined with a growing talent for acting, made of the part she played, an exquisite portrayal of Spanish aristocracy grown old in love and romance." Moryck was more critical of Regina's fellow actors, stating that they gave Andrews "adequate support" and that her acting "covered all other defects, and carried the play." Moryck concluded her review by stating that she "prophesies a future for Mrs. Andrews, both as actress and playwright."[27]

Regina also appeared as Madame Pugeot in the play *Queens of France*, a Creole play about New Orleans in 1872 directed by Harold Jackman.[28] This performance took place at the YWCA auditorium at 144 W. 135th Street, a new venue for the HET, and no admission fee was charged.[29]

Regina also starred in the production of *The Duchess Says Her Prayers*. The acting received positive although not effusive praise: "Ira De A. Reid and Mrs. Regina Anderson Andrews gave very competent performances." The reviewer did acknowledge the guest artist Edna Thomas as Madonna for her beauty and noted that "she read the delicately subtle lines of the play with a fine sense of feeling." The period costumes were described as "richly handsome." However, the setting and lighting were described as "poor and detracted from what was otherwise a charming play." Reid, like Regina, was not a professional actor. He was "[a]n eminent sociologist, educator, veteran, Quaker, activist, and *Opportunity* editor known for his invaluable research on African-American life and experience."[30] Thomas, on the other hand, acted in many theater productions including *The Emperor Jones* with Paul Robeson and starred as Lady MacBeth in Orson Welles's acclaimed version of *Macbeth* for the Negro Unit of the Federal Theater Project. Thomas auditioned for the role of Peola in the 1934 version of *Imitation of Life*. The role was awarded to her friend Fredi Washington, but both Thomas and Washington "shared the common dilemma of being black actors who did not look or sound black enough for unimaginative casting directors."[31] Thomas played the Mexican flower vendor in both the stage and screen versions of *A Streetcar Named Desire* with Marlon Brando and Jessica Tandy on stage and Brando and Vivian Leigh on screen. Thomas was not the only noted actress to be involved with the HET. Hilda Simms, who began her career at the Harlem Experimental Theatre, starred on Broadway in *Anna Lucasta*.[32]

The No 'Count Boy was on the same bill with *The Duchess Says Her Prayers*. The reviewer was particularly critical of the acting in *The No 'Count Boy*, noting that the lead had "an extreme tendency to overact; too many sobs in his voice and always playing to the audience." The two other actors including playwright and set designer Robert Dorsey "were at times self-consciously amused with their acting." Although critical of Dorsey's acting, the reviewer noted that "the high spot in the presentation of this play was the charmingly beautiful setting" constructed by Dorsey.[33] The anonymous reviewer would not be the last person to praise Dorsey for this particular skill. Unfortunately, photographic evidence of Dorsey's scenery does not exist due to an unfortunate turn of events.

The pseudonymous Basil Winters, a reviewer for the *Chicago Defender*, had a different reaction to both plays. He agreed with the previous reviewer of *The Duchess Says Her Prayers* that the guest artist Edna Thomas was beautiful and "her trained art lent distinction to the performance." He noted that "Regina Anderson Andrews as the 'Duchess' was moving in her supplication to retain her husband's love. Ira De A. Reid played the duke with nobility of character. The subtlety of lines demanded by this one-act play was not always achieved; often the lines were misplaced and the impression meant to be left eluded the audience. It would be much better to stick to plays like the second presentation."[34]

Unlike the previous anonymous reviewer, Winter liked *The No 'Count Boy*. He noted that it was perfectly cast and the direction was better. Of the lead he said that he "brought to the principal role an imaginative freshness." He called Robert Dorsey "splendid" and praised Dorsey's setting stating, "Robert Dorsey deserves special credit for his interesting setting. Handicapped by a very small stage, he overcame this by using a gauze curtain to create an effect of distance."[35]

The following year a review of three HET plays began with the critique that "[a]lthough the plays were in the most instances well performed, it was an unbalanced selection, since they were all more or less of the same type. None of the plays had enough action, being rather passive in their emotional quality." The reviewer, Edward Perry, noted that all of the conversation in the three forty-minute plays became tedious. He first reviewed *A Sunny Morning* starring Regina, whom he applauded for "an enchanting performance. . . . Her interpretation of the part was done with charming grace." He also said her costume was lovely and commended the acting of Robert Dorsey, noting that he gave "a fine performance" in *The Rider of Dreams,* and noted that the playwright, Ridgeley Torrence, was in the audience. Torrence, a white Ohio native, had lived among African Americans, and his plays "represented Negroes as serious folk characters."[36]

The final play of the evening was Regina's *Climbing Jacob's Ladder*, which Perry did not enjoy. He noted that the story "might have been more interesting if the author hadn't attempted to be so photographic in having so many speeches, which became ever so boring before a climax was finally reached." Once again, Dorsey was singled out for the setting. Perry noted that he "created a beautiful set for 'A Sunny Morning.' In this branch of the arts this young man has great talent which deserves to be encouraged."[37]

The *Chicago Defender* published another article about the same three plays, although it did not go into great detail. It mainly noted their existence, but the reviewer did say that "[a]ll of the plays were well presented and especially good was 'Climbing Jacob's Ladder.'"[38]

Brenda Ray Moryck reviewed the trio of plays for the *New York Age*. She also noted that the playwright was in attendance and "gave the production his unstinted praise." As for the play, Moryck said, "[a]s a whole, 'The Rider of Dreams' was good, but the grouping of characters can be improved, and the movement of the action speeded up if it would measure up to what the production can be." In reference to *A Sunny Morning*, Moryck observed that it "is a play requiring but two major characters, therefore the success of its performance depends almost entirely upon the players. There is little in the lines that is either novel or inspiring, yet the play has charm in the extreme." She praised Regina's performance but was critical of her costar, James Thibadeaux, whom she described as "an unequal opposite for her." Although he was dressed as an elderly person, "his young gestures and mannerisms and the intonations of his voice from which he could not keep the virility of youth, completely betrayed him." She credited Robert Dorsey with designing a "pretty setting."[39]

Both the *Chicago Defender* and the *New York Age* reviews mentioned the audience, the *Chicago Defender* noting that about three hundred people were in the audience.[40] This is the only article to note the size of the audience so we have no way of knowing if this was the usual attendance level. The *New York Age* article mentioned that Regina's play "captured its critical audience of Negroes and Nordics." So unlike the mandate from the KRIGWA Players to produce plays "for us," the HET performed in front of an interracial audience with "Nordics," no doubt referencing white people and not Scandinavians. No one noted the audience's socioeconomic status, which would be difficult to gauge just from appearances, but the tickets cost fifty cents during the Depression. Were people willing to spend that amount on plays? Perhaps the plays provided an escape from the drudgery of their lives, although most of the HET productions were not comedies.

The two plays created in Paul Glick's playwriting class, Andrews's *Underground* and Robert Dorsey's *Waxen Lily*, shared the bill with *Eviction*, about which the reviewer noted that "[t]he construction of this play was weak. . . . The author failed to reach his point." But two of the actors "did a fine piece of acting." Of Dorsey's *Waxen Lily*, the author stated, "A strangely impressive atmosphere pervades the plays and is quite skillfully developed. The audience's attention was held tense throughout this performance. . . . Miss Lewis, by her great dramatic ability took all honors of the evening for her wonderful performance." Oddly, Regina's play *Underground* was not reviewed. The reviewer noted only that the director also appeared in the cast of the play. Overall the reviewer concluded about the trio of plays: "None of the parts were stilted because of lack of feeling. There was a freedom of action and love of drama which carried the Harlem Experimental Players in the hearts of everyone who witnessed the performances."[41]

Goat Alley was the next play reviewed and described as "one of the pioneer plays dealing with Race Life . . . the struggle of a girl to retain the one true love in her life against the odds of loneliness and poverty."[42] The play was directed by Irish American dramatist John O'Shaughnessey, who was formerly involved with professional theater groups in Seattle, Washington. Like Paul Glick's playwriting class, O'Shaugnessey's participation demonstrated that the HET was beginning to attract established theater professionals.

A review of *Goat Alley*, "a realistic but tragic portrait of life in Washington, D.C., ghettos,"[43] written by white playwright Ernest Howard Culbertson, praised the overall efforts of the HET's "compact loyal group of workers" and their "increasing skill in the art of production." The acting was labeled as "superb," and director O'Shaughnessey was praised for his guidance. Dorsey "once more proved a craftsman in the set." The costume design and lighting was also singled out for admiration.[44]

Although the productions were far from perfect, there is no doubt that the HET members put a lot of effort into the staging of the plays. Rehearsals were on Monday, Wednesday, and Thursday evenings; during the workweek when most of the members of HET were employed doing other work to pay the bills, Regina worked as a librarian.[45]

*   *   *

Regina wrote three one-act plays under the pseudonym Ursala/Ursula Trelling—not a well-kept secret. Feminist scholar Carolyn Heilbrun noted that women were more likely to create pseudonyms than men noting that "women have long searched, and continue to search, for an identity 'other' than their own. Caught in the conventions of their sex, they have sought an escape from gender."[46] All of the lead characters in Regina's plays were male, which was not common for the female playwright.[47] She never said why she wrote from a male perspective. Perhaps she too was searching for another identity separate from Regina the responsible and sensible librarian. In a letter to her friend Freeman she recalls living in Normal, Illinois, and noting that "those memories all seem strangely incongruous with New York, and the 'Regina' whom I am best acquainted with now."[48]

Theater scholars noted Regina's plays "touch on key tropes in African American experience and imagination."[49] Such common themes included lynching[50] and passing—black characters who pretended to be white, usually for financial benefits and to live a more comfortable life. Passing was a common theme in Harlem Renaissance plays, short stories, and novels. Regina's plays were, "spare, moral, and realist one-act dramas . . . not set in the domestic feminist sphere, which was common, or almost mandatory, for women writers of any race at the time."[51]

Regina's play *Underground* was listed on a triple bill, and admission was fifty cents at St. Philips Parish House at 215 West 133rd Street in Harlem; curtain was 8:45 P.M., which made for a long night, with each one-act play lasting approximately forty minutes. The plays were performed on Thursday and Friday nights.

Underground tells the story of a family of runaway slaves—a mother, daughter, and stepfather—the biological father is believed to be the slave-owner—which accounts for the daughter's resemblance to the slaveowner's own daughter.[52] The family fools the bounty hunters into believing that their daughter is the slaveowner's daughter who is said to be in the area with two slaves. The family escapes from slavery.

Another play written by Regina was *The Man Who Passed*.[53] Often, in African American literature, the person who was passing was female—unlike Andrews's male protagonist, Fred Carrington. There is no evidence that this play was ever performed so there are no known reviews.

A possible inspiration from this play was the tale of the brother of Regina's roommate, Ethel Ray Nance. Ethel said that she never considered passing because, "I've always been very conscious of the fact of being Negro." However, her sibling did pass, and she recalled, "[m]y oldest brother, who made the other choice, told me at the time of my father's funeral, that he felt that I had made the best choice. At least, I've been able to live a rather natural life."[54]

The action takes place in a barbershop located in the basement of a building in Harlem where Carrington has come to get his hair styled. A newsboy stops by the barbershop and Carrington purchases the local black newspaper from him. Suddenly Carrington looks shocked—his father's obituary is in the paper and it states that his father was grieving the death of his wife who died three weeks earlier. Carrington, who has lost both his parents, reveals that it was his father who stopped speaking to him when he married his white wife. Heartbroken, he says goodbye to his friend Joe, who has the last line, "poor debbil."

Regina's final play, *Climbing Jacob's Ladder*, was probably influenced by a childhood memory—the execution of her father's client Thomas Jennings. Antilynching advocate Ida B. Wells-Barnett unsuccessfully partnered with Regina's father to try to save Jenning's life. Regina said:

> Before coming to New York, I had been very much influenced by Ida B. Wells Barnett. . . . When I was a child in Chicago and first heard of lynchings, they were incomprehensible. It's understandable that in my twenties I would have to write a play about lynching.[55]

Climbing Jacob's Ladder[56] premiered at St. Philip's Parish House in Harlem on April 24, 1931. This is Regina's most well-known play and is often cited in recent literature examining black women playwrights.

This play was among other lynching dramas written during this time period, including *Rachel* by Angelina Grimke and *A Sunday Morning in the
South* by Georgia Douglas Johnson. Grimke was born in Boston in 1880 into
a privileged and distinguished family. Grimke, named after her great-aunt
Angelina Grimke, a white abolitionist, was a poet, teacher, and playwright.
Her antilynching play, was inspired by her family's activism. *Rachel*, Grimke's
most renowned play, was about a woman who vows never to marry or to
bring children into this racist world. Regina most likely was in the audience
when the KRIGWA Players performed this drama.

The setting of *Climbing Jacob's Ladder* is a church described as "a shabby
little place of worship in an outlying Negro district in the South" on a Wednesday evening. The setting itself is unusual because most lynching plays were
set in the home.[57] A young black man, Wash Thomas, is in trouble and the
meeting is about how to raise $300 for his defense. While the congregation
of two local churches argue about who should be on the committee to make
decisions about the distributions of the funds raised by the two churches, one
parishioner, Sammy, hears noises and steps outside. When Sammy returns
he informs the congregation that Wash Thomas has been lynched.

Climbing Jacob's Ladder was originally titled *Down in Yamacraw*, according
to W. E. B. Du Bois's letter providing criticism on her play. He wrote, "The boy
who brings the news makes a dramatic entry, and then a rather long speech. I
doubt if this will do. My judgment is therefore that in its present form the play
would not take, but that if a climax could be arranged, and if you had rather
exceptional actors, it might make an excellent one-act play."[58] After Du Bois
attended a performance he wrote to Regina, "I saw your play last night but
had to hurry off before getting a chance to speak to you. . . . [Y]our play, was
thrilling. I enjoyed it immensely, and it gripped the audience. Congratulations
on it. Sometime we'll talk it over."[59]

Theater critic Brenda Ray Moryck wrote, "[t]he setting was perfect, the
acting the best of the evening, the movement swift and pertinent." Moryck
quoted another writer in the audience, drama critic and anthologist, Pierre
Loving, who said "the play ranks well with any of the already published one-
act plays and prophesies a future for Mrs. Andrews."[60]

Korithia Mitchell's dissertation about lynching dramas included an extensive analysis of Regina's play's critical religious themes. She concluded,
"Andrews suggested community activism based in religion often failed to
help black victims. . . . The play suggests that blacks, especially religious ones,
expend their energy in ways that ensure their continued victimization."[61] A
dramatic scene from the play was published in the July 1931 issue of *Crisis*.[62]

During this time period Regina met Russian author Boris Pil'njak, who
spent six months in the United States in 1931. He later wrote a fictional ac-

count about his experiences in *Okay, An American Novel*. The novel included a section about Boris meeting Regina and other African Americans in Harlem. Regina's friend and possible former paramour Joseph Freeman served as Pil'njak's interpreter during his stay, which included a visit to Hollywood, where Pil'njak wrote a script for MGM studio. In a letter written on October 3, 1931, from Moscow to Freeman, Pil'njak wrote:

> Call Ella Winter and get her to track down the black Regina. And when will Regina come to USSR? Bring her with you! Tell her that if she comes, I'll marry her. Seriously, I mean it. We are going to write plays together, she will teach me how to. I am totally serious about this. I love Regina very much.

Ella Winter was a journalist who wrote about Russia.[63] Perhaps Boris was unaware of Joseph's previous "relationship" with Regina. Also, not only was Regina married during this time but Boris was married to one of his three wives. Later in the same letter he encourages Joseph to come to Russia and to "Bring Regina! Or, who knows, I'll get tired of waiting for her and, following your lead, I'll engage in the same kind of standardized procedures as you did on such a scale in California, New York, and Mexico."[64] Reading between the lines we can infer that Pil'njak was referring to sexual liaisons. We have no way of knowing whether Regina and Boris ever had more than friendship, but there is evidence that he was enthralled with her. In *Okay, An American Novel*, Pil'njak recalled a time when he "visited a young dramatist, Regina Andrews, whose play was being presented at a Harlem theatre and whose husband was an attorney." He mentioned that she worked downtown "in the city of the whites" as a librarian. He remembered, "When I called upon her the first time, she, her husband and their friends were outside playing with a ball. The four of them were standing each one in a corner and they were passing the ball to each other."[65] No doubt that this was the first time that Pil'njak had ever met black people and he was intrigued; and yet his impressions were stereotypical. He declared, "What joyful, warm, comradely people are the Blacks! And what carefree people." There is no record of Regina ever going to Russia and no correspondence with Boris—perhaps because he could only write in Russian, as he did in his letter to Freeman. After his 1931 visit to the United States, he returned to Russia and was arrested in 1937, accused of being a traitor to the government. He was believed to be executed in 1938, although his family did not learn about his fate for decades.[66]

A few years after meeting Pil'njak, in June 1933, the HET prepared to present *Queen of France*, a play by white playwright Thornton Wilder, best known for his play *Our Town*. A September 1933 news article announced a roster of plays for the fifth season of the HET, but because there were no reviews of the plays or announcement of performances, it may be that the season never took place.[67] What is known is that the HET had plans to continue its tradition of mixing plays by both white and African American playwrights. They planned to stage white Nobel Laureate Eugene O'Neill's *The Dreamy Kid* and two plays by an African American playwright and a composer. Clarence Cameron White, an African American composer, wrote the musical compositions for *Tambour*. African American May Miller's play *Riding the Goat* was also scheduled for a performance. The play explored the "social roles of ritual, accommodation, and heroism. As a love story, the play also introduced a fearless heroine whose example inspires others to noble action."[68]

There is no indication about what caused the demise of the HET. It was probably difficult to maintain this activity when many of the members were self-taught amateurs with other work and family obligations.

Decades later, in 1980, the Audience Development Committee (AUDELCO), an organization in New York City dedicated to the African American theater, honored Regina with a pioneer award. Choreographer and actor Debbie Allen and dancer and actor Gregory Hines presided over the event. The awards were designed "to recognize the work of black theatrical artists and their work, sometimes overlooked because it takes place outside of the mainstream of the theater."[69] Perhaps, moved by the ceremony and honor, Regina decided to donate the HET scrapbooks to AUDELCO instead of including them with the papers and photograph collections that she would soon donate to the Schomburg Center for Research in Black Culture. Unfortunately, these scrapbooks are lost. In 1990, the offices of AUDELCO were ransacked and several priceless items were stolen including, according to Vivian Robinson, AUDELCO's founder and director, items from Regina Andrews.[70] The only known photographs of HET productions are in Regina's print and photograph collection at the Schomburg Center for Research in Black Culture and the photograph from *Climbing Jacob's Ladder* published in *Crisis*. However, a recent movement to recover lost writings to demonstrate the contributions of black female playwrights by black feminist scholars has recognized Regina's contributions to black women's writing and has included two of her plays in anthologies and included her in entries in bibliographies and dictionaries about black writers.[71] Theater scholars Kathy A. Perkins and Judith L. Stephens declared, "Andrews was instrumental in helping to nurture the Little Negro Theatre Movement in Harlem."[72]

While Regina's work with the Harlem Experimental Theatre was creatively fulfilling, she faced problems in the workplace caused by the racially restrictive employment policies of the New York Public Library.

Portrait of Regina Andrews. Photo courtesy Photographs and Prints Division, Schomburg Center for Research in Black Culture, The New York Public Library.

Regina's father William Grant "Habeas Corpus" Anderson. Photo courtesy Photographs and Prints Division, Schomburg Center for Research in Black Culture, The New York Public Library.

Regina's mother Margaret Simons Anderson Moore. Photo courtesy Photographs and Prints Division, Schomburg Center for Research in Black Culture, The New York Public Library.

Regina's maternal family—Portrait of the Simons Family in Normal, Illinois. Photo courtesy Photographs and Prints Division, Schomburg Center for Research in Black Culture, The New York Public Library.

Regina's brother Maurice Barton Anderson. Photo courtesy Photographs and Prints Division, Schomburg Center for Research in Black Culture, The New York Public Library.

Regina's sister Mercedes Alice Anderson. Photo courtesy Photographs and Prints Division, Schomburg Center for Research in Black Culture, The New York Public Library.

Regina's maternal Aunt Kate. Photo courtesy Photographs and Prints Division, Schomburg Center for Research in Black Culture, The New York Public Library.

Young Regina Anderson. Photo courtesy Photographs and Prints Division, Schomburg Center for Research in Black Culture, The New York Public Library.

Regina's maternal grandfather Reverend Henry Simons and his second wife Laura. Photo courtesy Photographs and Prints Division, Schomburg Center for Research in Black Culture, The New York Public Library.

The Simons's family home at 405 North Fell Avenue, Normal, Illinois. Photo courtesy Photographs and Prints Division, Schomburg Center for Research in Black Culture, The New York Public Library.

Regina Anderson. Photo courtesy Photographs and Prints Division, Schomburg Center for Research in Black Culture, The New York Public Library.

Guests at breakfast party for Langston Hughes hosted by Regina Anderson and Ethel Ray at 580 St. Nicholas Avenue, Harlem. Back row, left to right: Ethel Ray, Langston Hughes, Helen Lanning, Pearl Fisher, Rudolph Fisher, Louella Tucker, Clarissa Scott, Hubert Delany. Front row, left to right: Regina Anderson, Esther Popel, Jessie Fauset, Marie Johnson, and E. Franklin Frazier. Photo courtesy Photographs and Prints Division, Schomburg Center for Research in Black Culture, The New York Public Library.

Langston Hughes (far left) with (left to right) Charles S. Johnson, E. Franklin Frazier, Rudolph Fisher, and Hubert T. Delany, on the roof of 580 St. Nicholas Avenue, Harlem. Photo courtesy Photographs and Prints Division, Schomburg Center for Research in Black Culture, The New York Public Library.

William "Bill" Trent Andrews Jr. and Regina. Photo courtesy Photographs and Prints Division, Schomburg Center for Research in Black Culture, The New York Public Library.

William Trent Andrews Sr., Regina's father-in-law. Photo courtesy Photographs and Prints Division, Schomburg Center for Research in Black Culture, The New York Public Library.

Husband William T. Andrews delivering address. Photo courtesy Photographs and Prints Division, Schomburg Center for Research in Black Culture, The New York Public Library.

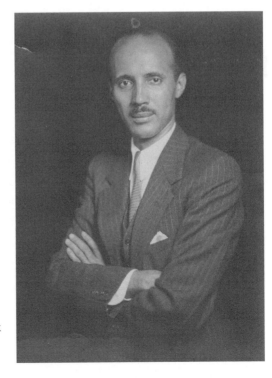

Husband William Trent Andrews Jr. Photo courtesy Photographs and Prints Division, Schomburg Center for Research in Black Culture, The New York Public Library.

Scene from the Harlem Experimental Theatre production of *The Duchess Says Her Prayers* with Edna Lewis Thomas (left), Ira De Augustine Reid, and Regina Anderson Andrews. Photo courtesy Photographs and Prints Division, Schomburg Center for Research in Black Culture, The New York Public Library. (Credit: Richards-Ward Photo Studio)

Scene from the Harlem Experimental Theatre production of *Climbing Jacob's Ladder* by Regina Andrews. Photo courtesy Photographs and Prints Division, Schomburg Center for Research in Black Culture, The New York Public Library. (Credit: Campbell)

William T. Andrews, Regina Andrews, and Regina Ann Andrews (daughter). Photo courtesy Photographs and Prints Division, Schomburg Center for Research in Black Culture, The New York Public Library.

William T. Andrews and daughter Regina Ann Andrews, Mahopac, New York. Photo courtesy Photographs and Prints Division, Schomburg Center for Research in Black Culture, The New York Public Library.

Langston Hughes signing autographs (Regina Andrews, right) at the Washington Heights Branch of the New York Public Library as part of the Family Night at the Library series. Photo courtesy Photographs and Prints Division, Schomburg Center for Research in Black Culture, The New York Public Library.

Regina Andrews (far right) and unidentified guest speakers during a Family Night at the Library program at the Washington Heights Branch of the New York Public Library. Photo courtesy Photographs and Prints Division, Schomburg Center for Research in Black Culture, The New York Public Library.

6. The New York Public Library

All was not well in Regina's professional life. For all that she was doing for the New York Public Library, Regina believed that she was neither being paid a wage that recognized her contributions nor being afforded the opportunities for promotion she deserved. Her relationship with Ernestine Rose deteriorated as Regina frequently asked W. E. B. Du Bois, representing the National Association for the Advancement of Colored People (NAACP), to intervene on her behalf with the NYPL administration.[1] A family friend and former client of Regina's father, defense attorney William G. "Habeas Corpus" Anderson of Chicago, Du Bois commonly went over Rose's head, first to Franklin H. Hopper and later to Francis R. St. John, the chiefs of the NYPL Circulation Department who were in charge of the branch libraries.[2]

In order to understand Du Bois's involvement with Regina we need to examine his earlier dispute with the NYPL administration on behalf of librarian Catherine Latimer—the first African American librarian in the system.[3] Du Bois frequently battled New York City institutions such as the Harlem Hospital and the public school system, which repeatedly denied highly educated, middle-class African Americans hiring opportunities—or, if hired, the African Americans would not receive desirable opportunities for promotion. Du Bois was particularly galled by the situation at NYPL, which limited African American librarians to a few branches.[4]

Catherine Latimer was born around 1895 in Nashville and educated at Howard University and Columbia University's library school. She came to the 135th Street Branch in 1920 after working as a library assistant at Tuskegee Institute. Latimer was the reference librarian in charge of the Negro Literature and History collection at the branch. After the Carnegie Corporation gave the NYPL a $10,000 grant to purchase Puerto Rican–born bibliophile Arturo Schomburg's collection of Negro literature and history, Schomburg was named curator of the collection—a move that Latimer felt threatened her position at the 135th Street Branch.

Du Bois wrote to other community leaders, including Reverend Lloyd Imes of Harlem's St. James Presbyterian Church; George Schuyler, a prominent newspaper columnist; Reverend Adam Clayton Powell Sr., the influential leader of Harlem's Abyssinian Baptist Church and Community House; and Regina's future mentor Eugene Kinckle Jones, the executive secretary of the National Urban League's New York City office.[5]

A group that included Du Bois and his wife (Nina), Reverend Imes and his wife (Grace), Jones, and two other women met with Hopper and Rose in January 1932 at the 42nd Street Branch. Du Bois opened the meeting by stating that colored people educated their children so that they could receive certain employment opportunities. However, these children often faced discrimination, which he implied might be expected when dealing with "prejudiced whites" but not educated whites. He also mentioned the lack of African American employees at the 135th Street Branch. Du Bois noted that the library did not seem interested in hiring and keeping "competent colored library assistants." The meeting concluded with Hopper and Rose reiterating that they were interested in employing the services of "a larger number of well-trained, efficient and upstanding colored assistants," and the committee members offered to provide the NYPL with eligible candidates.[6]

Several months later Latimer sent Du Bois a much more positive letter, stating, "Your recent conference downtown certainly had some effect!" She told Du Bois that the 135th Street Branch now had three librarians on staff, three substitutes not including Schomburg, three librarians involved in the Adult Education program, and two junior clerks, for a total of twelve colored workers on the staff at that branch.[7] Things were looking up at the NYPL in 1932. Although no longer at the same branch, Regina and Latimer were both Third Grade Assistants, with Latimer receiving higher wages because she was at the grade longer than Regina.[8] However, the path that Regina took to obtain this promotion was not easy.

After dispensing with Latimer's case against the NYPL, Du Bois took up the fight against the NYPL on behalf of Regina. He minced few words. In one such meeting with Hopper and Rose on December 23, 1929, he asked Hopper when or if "X," as Du Bois referred to Regina in his notes, was going to be promoted to Third Grade Library Assistant? Hopper assured him that Regina would receive a promotion and that he understood her impatience with the delay but said delays were not unusual. Hopper noted that in order for Regina to be promoted to Third Grade, she had to receive recommendations from two librarians who were willing to receive her as first assistant. Regina had received a recommendation from Leah Lewinson at the 115th Street Branch and from Ernestine Rose at the 135th Street Branch. However, Rose said she might instead hire Regina for the position of Second First Assistant, which Du Bois characterized as "unusual," since no such position existed. Rose also indicated that if there were an opening she couldn't guarantee that it would go to Regina. In reply, Du Bois "reminded H.[Hopper] of color prejudice; of our natural fear that it had crept in this case and of the difficulty which we are always under of suspecting prejudice when it was not present or later it became entrenched when it was present . . . [t]hat in the latter case, there was nothing for us to do but to fight."

Admitting that there was prejudice in the communities served by the local libraries and among the staff regarding colored people, Jews, and Italians, Hopper nevertheless assured Du Bois that color prejudice was not the case with Regina and that when Regina's name came before the board her color was not designated. Hopper continued that he thought prejudice was decreasing except toward the Jews. Du Bois replied firmly "that such a situation, while natural, must not be left to drift. It needed active, although tactful, attack." The meeting ended with Hopper assuring Du Bois that Regina eventually would receive an appointment.[9]

Not satisfied, on February 18, 1930, Du Bois wrote Ferdinand Q. Morton, a Democratic leader in Harlem and a successful lawyer, formerly an assistant district attorney in New York County, that he (Du Bois) was ready to battle the NYPL system. "For a long time no Negroes were admitted at all," he informed Morton, adding:

> Mrs. Andrews has done her work well, and yet she has had to fight every inch of the way. She has continually been doing, as she is now, the work of higher grade, while being paid for a lower grade. . . . It seems to me that it is high time for an investigation into this situation.[10]

Then Du Bois sent blistering letters to both Hopper and Rose:[11]

> You say that you recommended Mrs. Andrews for appointment in the Third Grade [he addressed Rose]. But Mr. Hopper told me that you particularly qualified that by saying that you would not obligate yourself to receive her as your First Assistant, and I understand that this qualification really invalidated the recommendation as such recommendation must carry with it the willingness of the Branch Librarian to receive the one recommended as her Assistant. No one is asking for the compulsory transfer of any present First Assistant, but whereas there are forty-two branches in the New York system where white librarians

may be appointed, apparently there are only one or two where the color line permits a colored Assistant. It seems to me, to say the least, that vacancies in those libraries should be made available for qualified colored girls. Of course, this, however, is only the beginning. The whole system by which colored girls are kept from appointment in other libraries should be swept away. I do not agree with you that you have been "conscious of the libraries need of adequately prepared colored Assistants." I think, on the contrary, that you and the library authorities have made no real effort to get such assistance and that their appearance has been a cause of embarrassment to you. But I do trust that in the future this attitude is going to change.

To Hopper, Du Bois wrote:

[T]his library situation in New York, so far as colored persons are concerned, has reached a pass where concerted and determined action is called for. . . . Mrs. Andrews has been in the system since 1925 [actually, 1923] and has been in line for the position which she is now seeking since 1926. While she has been waiting for the chance to qualify, several others who had the chance to qualify after she was ready, have received promotion. . . . [W]hile apparently there are forty-two branches where white assistants may get their experience and promotion, there are only two or three where colored girls will be tolerated.

Worst of all, Du Bois concluded, "the system of promotion and appointments is made to depend to an extraordinary degree upon the whims and prejudices of Branch Librarians and that what is needed is a broad system of Civil Service tests which will give a more democratic flavor to a great city institution."

Others joined Du Bois in protest. On February 20, 1930, his colleague, Walter White, then acting secretary of the NAACP,[12] boycotted the library on Regina's behalf and wrote Rose:

Yesterday I wrote, tentatively agreeing to speak as you requested on March 5th to the Library School students in and about New York. This morning, for the first time, I have learned of the efforts which my associate, Dr. Du Bois, has been making in behalf of Mrs. Regina Andrews, who apparently has been denied, on account of color prejudice, opportunity for advancement in the New York Public Library. Under the circumstances, I do not feel that I care to speak at the library until this situation is settled satisfactorily, not only with regard to Mrs. Andrews but until barriers based on color prejudice are removed from the path of any colored person in the New York Public Library system.[13]

The fictional Regina, Carl Van Vechten's librarian Mary Love in *Nigger Heaven*, also discussed her poor treatment in the library system where she worked. Mary's roommate Olive exclaimed, "'Why, Mary,' she protested. 'Do you get along? Don't you get less salary than white girls and aren't white girls without half your experience or ability promoted over you?'"[14] Later, the character Adora declared, "You're a librarian, but you'll never get as much pay as the white librarians. They won't even put you in charge of a branch library. Not because you're not as good as the others—probably you're better—but because you're coloured."[15] Perhaps Van Vechten had been privy to these conversations between Regina and others at her salon, though Regina may have been reluctant to share her impressions of color prejudice in front of a white man. Perhaps Van Vechten's affinity with the African American artists made it okay.

Three and a half months after the confrontation, on June 10, 1930, Regina received a telegram notifying her "that you have been transferred from the 135th Street Branch to Rivington Street Branch and . . . [promoted] from Grade 2 to Grade 3, as assistant branch librarian, with an increase in salary from $155 to $165 per month, dating from June 1."[16] The outcome was reported in *Crisis*, "Mrs. Regina Andrews, after a plucky fight, is First Assistant at the Rivington Branch."[17] With this satisfactory conclusion, Du Bois turned his attention to others needing his advocacy, and Regina went about her new job. However, neither was done with the NYPL administration yet.

As if Regina did not have enough things to concern her at work, she became aware of problems back in Normal, Illinois, with the family homestead. It would not be the last time that Regina found herself being pulled back into a family fray.

When Regina's maternal grandfather, Rev. Henry Simons, died, he left his home to his family. There was no mortgage left; however, at some point, Regina's mother returned to live there, but the taxes fell into arrears. Regina wrote a letter to a Mr. Faull. His relationship to the house is unclear. Perhaps he was a tax collector. Regina informed Faull that she had provided her mother with some financial support to maintain the property in Normal, Illinois, and to support her niece, Maurice's daughter, who was being raised by her mother. Regina suggested that she and her Aunt Kate could pay him $25 a month. She concluded by stating:

> I receive no income from the Normal property; but have assumed some of my mother's obligations there for a number of years. It is too far away to be of any comfort to my husband or to me. Having heavy expenses here, you can see why we hesitate to assume an obligation so far removed from us.[18]

The house was saved, but over a decade later, Regina's Aunt Kate would return to live at 405 North Fell Avenue, resulting in a dispute with Regina's mother. While Regina was dealing with 405 North Fell Avenue, she was living at 405 Edgecombe Avenue in Harlem. The 409 Edgecombe Avenue building was the more prestigious building that comprised this "compound" but the

Andrewses' penthouse was almost certainly quite lovely too. During the 1930s and 1940s, luminaries of Harlem lived at 409 Edgecombe Avenue, including W. E. B. Du Bois, future leader of the NAACP Roy Wilkins, Walter White, Aaron Douglas, and future Supreme Court Justice Thurgood Marshall, among others.[19]

On December 1, 1936, Regina left the Rivington Street Branch and was transferred to the 115th Street Branch where she remained for over a decade.[20] During the month that Regina arrived at this branch, there was a "special exhibition of the work of three promising local Negro artists."[21] The artists were not named but Regina was likely involved with this exhibit and probably initiated it. This branch, like the 135th Street Branch, was serving "almost exclusively a colored community."[22]

During this time, the Works Progress Administration (WPA), an agency created by President Franklin D. Roosevelt to fund employment opportunities for Americans, financed the building of an auditorium dubbed the Little Theatre in the basement of this branch. Nine other branches also had little theaters.[23] The 115th Street Branch's grand opening took place on November 3, 1938, and on that occasion, Regina gave a speech as the Acting Branch Librarian, a new position she gained upon the retirement of Leah Lewinson. The celebration not only honored the opening of the auditorium and Little Theatre and Lewinson's retirement, but it celebrated Regina's groundbreaking promotion. She became the first African American to head a branch in NYPL history.[24] In her speech she said, "We must be more than Librarians, bibliophiles, curators and catalogers in order to develop the kind of social philosophy necessary for a modern community library."[25] She also stated that it was important to provide the community space for various activities such as clubs, lectures, classes, and plays—which she would later arrange. The branches were filled with lots of activities and were open daily from nine in the morning until nine at night for six days, closed on Sundays, for a total of seventy-two hours of services per week.[26] Of course, most patrons primarily visited the libraries for books, and during this time all of the branches were suffering from a "lack of books," a shortage of duplicates for popular books, and both the patrons and the library staff were increasingly frustrated with the long waiting lists.[27]

In 1938, Hopper informed Regina that he was appointing her to Acting Branch Librarian to prepare her to qualify for promotion to Grade 4. If she would submit three subjects for a thesis, he would present these to a local examining board for approval as part of her Grade 4 qualifications. Because many of the patrons at Regina's branch came from the American South and the West Indies, Regina wanted to "study library conditions and opportunities among Negroes in the rural regions of the South and also in certain Islands of the West Indies, particularly Spanish speaking ones." Hopper supported her search for a scholarship to support the research.[28] Regina's thesis ended up being about a different topic.

Before she completed the study, Regina received the good news that she received the promotion and a salary increase from $165 to $175 a month.[29] More than just a promotion, as a local paper reported, it represented a first:

> To Mrs. Regina Andrews of New York City goes the distinction of being the first Negro to be placed in full charge of a public library branch in the city of New York. Mrs. Andrews was appointed to head the branch at 201 West 115th Street recently, succeeding Miss Leah Lewinson who has retired. The branch is used by Columbia University students and by Negro and Spanish residents who make up the bulk of the population of the neighborhood.[30]

Accolades poured in. In addition to numbers of congratulatory messages, the Women's Service League of Brooklyn honored Regina with a medal at the 1939 World's Fair in New York City. In the company of illustrious women such as her good friend Jesse Fauset Harris (Literature), Dorothy Height (Religion), Augusta Savage (Sculpture), a very young Philippa Schuyler (Piano)[31] (daughter of George Schuyler), and Ethel Waters (The Stage), Regina was recognized for her work as a Supervising Librarian.[32]

A "colorful" tea was thrown in honor of Regina's appointment. The guests included noted children's librarian Miss Anne Caroll Moore, the supervisor of children's work.[33]

Regina described the 115th Street Branch in an article published in the *Chicago Defender*. She said:

> This particular branch offers unique opportunity for inter-racial library service. We have the largest collection of Spanish books in the city and have recently developed a fine collection of circulating books on the Negro. I feel that we have a splendid staff (12 full-time and six WPA workers) including Miss Pura Belpre in charge of children's work; Miss Mildred Gumaer in charge of the reference room and Miss Rose Zuvillaga in charge of the Spanish department. In October we will open to the public our new auditorium designed by WPA and equipped with all modern facilities for a little theatre. We anticipate an extremely busy and interesting season.

The reporter noted, "The branch she now heads is eighth in size and circulation of the group of city branches. Aside from her professional pursuits she is a member of Delta Sigma Theta sorority."[34]

Belpre, Regina's coworker mentioned in the article, was also a path-finder. She was the first Puerto Rican librarian to work for the NYPL.[35] Belpre was transferred from the Hamilton Grange Branch to the 115th Street Branch on December 1, 1938. Although Belpre was only at the branch for a short time before being transferred to the Aguilar Branch on September 14, 1939, the two women remained friends.[36]

Regina received numerous letters and telegrams from around the country congratulating her on this accomplishment. One letter came from Hubert T. Delany, who was one of the groomsmen at her wedding:

> I was delighted to hear of your recent and well deserved advancement as librarian in charge of the 115th Street Branch of the New York Public Library. You long ago deserved and merited this advancement. I am happy that, although late, it has come to you; and am encouraged to know that even in the New York Public Library, they will recognize unqualified merit when they see it.[37]

While Regina battled the NYPL, her husband fought discrimination and prejudice as an assemblyman representing Harlem and devoted his efforts to issues like education, welfare, and health that were impacting his African American constituents. Democrat party member Bill Andrews had entered political life a few years earlier. After working for five years, he was laid off by the NAACP in 1932 due to budget constraints.[38] He returned to private practice for the next three years before deciding to run for public office.[39] In 1935, he was elected as an assemblyman representing Harlem in the twenty-first district. Revealing some of his political interests, he was praised in the *New York Times* at the end of his first year as "[o]ne of the ablest and most independent and public-spirited of all the Assemblymen. His address in support of the child labor amendment was one of the finest in the session. He took an active interest in improving housing conditions." The annual appraisal by the Citizens Union concluded that Bill "gave his constituents distinguished representation."[40]

When Bill ran for assemblyman, part of his platform included a call for the "reapportionment of Congressional districts with a view of making possible the election of a Negro Congressman from Harlem." The reapportionment was done, and Bill would later campaign for this historic position. The African American press, both nationally and locally, particularly the *New York Amsterdam News*, assiduously recorded the battle for the seat in Congress and the various behind-the-scenes political machinations by powerful African American Democratic politicians. In August 1943, the current congressman representing the section of New York City that encompassed Harlem, Joseph A. Gavagan, announced that he would resign his seat in Congress after Labor

Day "to give Negroes in Harlem an opportunity to elect 'one of their own' in the November election. Early candidates included A. Phillip Randolph, who was encouraged to run for the position. The "more practical" politicians considered Bill a viable candidate. Another name that was bandied about for over a year was City Councilman Reverend Adam Clayton Powell.[41] By November 1943, Julius J. Adams of the *New York Amsterdam News* reported, "The congressional race next year has become a consuming topic in Harlem, where it is almost sure a Negro will be elected from the new 21st District." Adams noted that Bill said, "he is in the race, and is there to stay."[42] By February 1944, both Bill and Dr. Channing H. Tobias, a senior secretary of the local YMCA, were "considered to be the Rev. Powell's chief adversaries for the seat." Powell's own church, the powerful Abyssinian Baptist Church, voted to give him "$10,000 for his campaign." Journalist Earl Brown noted that more seasoned politicians were not supportive of Powell because he did not "play the old army, clubhouse game of politics, except when he is the beneficiary"; because of the strength in numbers of the constituency that attended his church, Powell "can always take his case directly to the people, thereby by-passing, circumnavigating the politicos."[43] Powell eventually did receive the endorsement of the powerful Tammany Hall, New York County's Democratic organization. Despite this setback, Bill stated that he was still a candidate for congress and cited his "superior legislative experience."[44] However, the African American press continued to portray Bill as the underdog.[45] In November 1944, Powell became "the first Negro from New York to go to Congress."[46]

Just as Regina supported Bill's ultimately unsuccessful run for Congress, Bill supported his wife in terms of continuing both her career and her education and later her creative and her future civic endeavors. He did not seem to expect Regina to remain at home and have dinner waiting for him after work.

Regina got a second chance to explore her creative side through the theater arts. It had been several years since the demise of the Harlem Experimental Theatre, and Regina was still involved in the performing arts through her work as a librarian. Budding playwright Loften Mitchell met with Regina at the suggestion of actor and mentor Dick Campbell. They discussed using the basement of the 115th Street Branch as a theater to perform plays. Along with several others, Mitchell formed the Pioneer Drama Group. He wrote the plays for their first two performances: *Cocktails*, about a black man running for president, and *Cross Roads*, about the 1935 Harlem riots. He called his plays "ridiculous" and "crazy," but that did not prevent Andrews from attending opening night. Mitchell said "she got up and urged the audience members to go out and get more audiences."[47] Someone notified and complained to the NYPL administration that the theater group was selling tickets. Mitchell remembered Regina's response to the NYPL. He "was standing there in her office when she told the downtown bosses to go to hell." He mentioned how the janitor tried to extort the teenagers by doubling his cleaning fee to $4. Mitchell said, "[w]hat I heard Mrs. Andrews tell that man cannot be put in print. I do not want to embarrass her. Let me simply state that we continued to pay two dollars per night for performances."[48]

The theater group remained at the branch until 1939 when Mitchell went to college, then the Navy, and eventually to graduate school. He returned in 1946, and the group became the 115th Street People's Theatre and produced seven plays during the next two years, including his own *The Cellar* and *The Bancroft Dynasty*.[49] Once again the NYPL administration became involved, and Regina was told that the group could not sell tickets. Reluctantly, Mitchell and his group left and formed the Harlem Showcase Theatre located at 290 Lenox Avenue.

During this time, Regina's family suffered a loss with the death of her father-in-law. William Trent Andrews Sr. died in Baltimore in 1940. In his column, "As the Crow Flies," Du Bois reminisced about his impression of Andrews Sr.:

> I remember William Trent Andrews when he first came to Fisk in the last decade of the Nineteenth Century. He was tall and straight, soldierly in bearing, as became one who had begun his training at West Point. Of his experience in the army academy, he said little. It was years after, . . . that I understood why. It is a terrible trial—that of youth out into the world to withstand all along the bitter shafts of race hate. Win or lose, they emerge marked for life. Never again for them is the fine, free faith in human kind. Their life must henceforth become a grim fight without quarter. Fine it is, if such a man saves his soul sufficiently to work doggedly on, to lift up new ideals, never to falter. Andrews lies dead in Baltimore, in his eighth decade, having earned a living, raised two worthy sons, talked plainly in his printed word, and he died, at last, sword in hand.

Maybe Bill inherited money from his father's estate that allowed them to purchase, in 1941, a 1799 New England style–home on thirty-four acres in Mahopac, New York, in Putnam County to use as a weekend retreat when Bill worked in Albany as an assemblyman. Mahopac has been described as "richly laced with lakes and streams and densely wooded hillsides."[50] Mahopac, also known as Lake Mahopac, "was originally settled by the Wappingers, one of the Algonquin Indian tribes. During the French and Indian War, the tribe traveled north to Massachusetts to fight for the British. When they returned, they found their territory had been taken over by colonists."[51] Earlier, "in the late 1800s [it] was primarily a summer resort of small cottages and some grand estates built around the main lake."[52]

Regina described the location of the home as "a very convenient meeting place. He would come down and I would come up" from New York City. The commute took approximately one hour. The home was in a state of disrepair when they purchased it, and they worked hard on getting it in a livable condition. The roof had caved in, the toilet was outside, and the house was heated by a little coal stove. Once restored, the Andrews entertained politicians in their home. Regina said that "I enjoyed going up there" to Albany because once a year the wives of all the assemblymen were honored.

A 1944 card, resembling something one might send friends and family at Christmas, showed Regina and Bill in their winter clothes standing in front of their home. Regina is holding their Persian cat, Nubbins, and the caption said that "Bill does all the planting" and Regina "cans and needlepoints." Further, it stated that "Bill is an inveterate pipe smoker and likes his spaghetti. He gets real pleasure out of farming on their 34 acre estate." The final sentence noted that they had no children—that would come later.

Regina continued to work at the 115th Street Branch but was dissatisfied with her compensation. The NYPL administration seemed to be very pleased with the programs and services that Regina provided at her branch. Hopper wrote, "You are to be congratulated in creating such willing cooperation from your staff. The Forums and the other activities in your Little Theatre sound most interesting and well-planned."[53]

In 1945, Regina completed her thesis, "A Public Library Assists in Improving Race Relations." The main research question was: "Can we as librarians extend the use to which books and working with books can create another road to racial understanding?"[54] Regina saw "the use of books as our strongest means of promoting intercultural understanding."[55]

Francis R. St. John, Hopper's replacement as the new chief of circulation, and the Advisory Board approved the thesis; in 1946, Regina was promoted to Grade 4.[56] To ensure that her new supervisor appreciated both who she was and the contribution she was making, after becoming Supervising Librarian, Regina asked St. John to write Du Bois detailing her record of accomplishment at NYPL. St. John wrote:

> In any evaluation of the community work which is being done in Harlem, I am certain that the contribution which Mrs. Andrews has made, and is making, in that area would be recognized as outstanding. . . . [S]ince 1940, [Andrews] has served as Branch Librarian, in which position she has well demonstrated her abilities as a responsible administrator. She has made the 115th Street Branch a real community center for the advancement of the work in which we are all so interested.[57]

Never one to miss an occasion to express his opinion, Du Bois put Regina's accomplishment in a larger context for St. John:

> I am glad to have this confirmation of my own estimate of Mrs. Andrews' work. I have known her over twenty years and was in some small way instrumental in making the fight by which the barrier against appointing a colored woman, even as first assistant much less librarian of a branch, was begun. My own impression has been that she was and is a most valuable worker, and for that reason I cannot understand why her salary should be the lowest paid any branch librarian; or why there is apparently no immediate prospect of her earning more in the near future.[58]

Regina transferred to the Washington Heights Branch in 1948 and adopted a child, Regina Ann.[59] Very little is available about the child's background; the circumstances surrounding the transaction, including the date and the reason, are unknown[60] A former library page who worked under Regina's supervision recalled the following about Regina Ann: "I knew she was adopted and . . . she appeared to have very little, but some, African blood."[61] Regina Ann, born January 22, 1945, thought that "she was adopted around 3." She believed that "she was left on a doorstep in Brooklyn NY" and that her birth name was Deitra Turner and her birth father was African American.[62] Regina Ann's daughter, Robyn, recalled, "people would see me with my mom and they would ask if I was adopted because [I] look nothing like her."[63] She added, "[T]o look at my mother you would think she was white."[64]

The Washington Heights Branch moved twice before settling at 1000 St. Nicholas Avenue in 1914, and it was located there when Regina began working at that branch; it remains there today. Like many other branches of the NYPL, that branch was designed by the architects Carrere and Hastings and was designed as a four-story building.

In the early 1950s, the branch served "Puerto Rican Americans, Americans of Jewish faith, Negro Americans, and many new citizens who came as refugees from Holland, Germany, Austria, and Poland." Patrons asked for foreign books in "German and French and very recently Spanish and Yiddish."[65] Decades earlier, in 1925, librarians noted the "intelligent use of the library" by "the first influx of Negroes settling in the area."[66]

As head of the Washington Heights Branch, Regina supervised a staff of ten, including an assistant librarian, Edna Law, who faced her own problems with NYPL as a Chinese woman and found a sympathetic boss in Regina. Other staff members included a children's librarian, a young adult librarian, two full-time and two part-time clerks, and three pages. Administrative duties included selecting and weeding books, periodicals, and newspapers in the 37,000-volume collection; training and promoting staff; and attending professional meetings. In addition, Regina secured speakers for Family Night at the Library,[67] which was a program she created. She imagined it was as if the library said to its patrons, "Come, meet your neighbor, and talk over with him those problems of living, learning, working, and playing together which, when frankly approached, will help to establish a well integrated community."[68]

A former page who worked for Regina at the Washington Heights Branch recalled, "I had the privilege of working for [Regina] as a library page while in high school. She was an elegant aristocrat. As devilish teens we were a handful and difficult to supervise."[69]

Although Regina was busy enough with her work and family responsibilities, she took on some civic commitments that would end up taking her around the world.

7. International Flights

Regina gave a speech at a Korean high-school graduation and recalled, "[A]fter I stopped speaking they got up and dashed out and I was so disappointed. I said (to myself) 'they didn't even stop to say that they like it or enjoyed it.' When I got outside they were all lined up in a long line all the way down to the road. That was almost a block and they were singing God Bless America. . . . I enjoyed Korea." This international travel opportunity was just one of several that Regina was able to benefit from through her civic work, including trips to Germany, Italy, China, Japan, India, Thailand, Pakistan, Lebanon, Afghanistan, Iran, Sierra Leone, Nigeria, Liberia, Ghana, Senegal, the Ivory Coast, and Brazil.[1]

One of the first civic organizations that Regina joined was the National Urban League in 1940. The Urban League was an interracial organization founded to help African Americans from the southern parts of the United States to transition to the north as part of the great migration. Many newcomers were victimized by discrimination and taken advantage of in terms of their housing and employment conditions. The Urban League helped people find adequate housing, enrolled children in schools, and offered job training and assistance. The middle-class African American members of the Urban League also offered classes about proper behavior in public, good hygiene, how to dress properly, and other lessons that could be condescending to the poor African Americans who took advantage of the services rendered by the organization.[2]

Of course Regina most likely felt a connection with the Urban League through her Harlem Renaissance roommate, Ethel Ray Nance, who worked for the house organ of the organization, *Opportunity* magazine. Perhaps Regina was interested in joining the National Urban League because of people like Eugene Kinckle Jones, who helped her with her career. Regina served on the League's board of trustees for twenty-two years under the directorships of Jones, Lester B. Granger, and Whitney Young. She was also a representative for the League at the United States Mission to the United Nations and as a member of the U.S. National Commission of the United Nations Educational, Scientific and Cultural Organization (UNESCO) from 1956 to 1959 and was reelected for a second term from 1959 to 1961. Regina described her role in UNESCO: "We members of the Commission have the responsibility of making recommendations for improving and expanding the facilities of education institutions, museums, and libraries around the world."[3]

Regina was easily able to participate in civic organizations while supervising the Washington Heights Branch. However, matters far away intruded into her life in New York City when she received a letter from her Aunt Kate concerning the family homestead at 405 North Fell Avenue in Normal, Illinois, and her mother, Margaret Moore.

Over a decade earlier, Regina and her Aunt Kate had saved the property from being seized for unpaid taxes. Now Aunt Kate resided there with Regina's mother, and all was not well. According to Aunt Kate, Regina's mother, whom she referred to as Mrs. M. (she was now Mrs. Fred Moore), had made plans to move several times and kept postponing her departure. However, in preparation for her departure, Margaret had begun selling or giving away various household items such as a sewing machine, garden tools, and the lawnmower, although Aunt Kate was to remain in the home and could use the items. There was also a dispute about who owned which items, with Aunt Kate insisting that some of them belonged to their parents. The other half of the dispute centered on students who rented rooms in the home. It was not uncommon for African American college students to rent rooms in local African American homes since they often were not allowed to board in the residence halls. One student who rented a room at 405 North Fell Avenue was Ida B. Wells-Barnett's granddaughter Lucille, who lived there around 1940.[4] Although Margaret had planned to leave before the summer school session began, she remained in Normal and collected rent from the students. Even more egregious to Kate, she collected and kept deposits for students entering the local colleges in the fall even though she had no intention of being there, and she hadn't asked her sister Kate if she wanted to have renters. Regina's Aunt Kate was enraged because she had helped to pay taxes and paid for repairs on the property while her sister Margaret reaped all of the benefits. Aunt Kate hoped to enlist Regina's help on the matter and expressed reluctance about involving Regina in the fracas, but she was at her wit's end. She ended her letter by stating, "I only want decent treatment Regina and *you* can help me to have it. . . . I shall not write again. Remember regardless to your feeling toward me—I still love you and Bill and wish you nothing but Good in every way."[5] It is unknown if or how the situation was resolved, but there would be no hard feelings between Regina and her Aunt Kate, who came to live with Regina a few decades later.

Meanwhile, in 1949, Regina's husband Bill, no longer an assemblyman, had returned to his law practice. He was also a member of the board of directors of Carver Federal Savings and Loan, Harlem's first African American loan institution.[6] Later, Bill resigned from the board in order to become their legal counsel.[7]

A year later, in 1950, at the time Regina created one of her proudest professional accomplishments, she suffered a very personal loss. Her father, William G. Anderson, died of a heart attack at the age of seventy-eight in his Chicago home at 3404 Vernon Avenue. As in life, his death was reported in both the African American and mainstream newspapers and his nickname "Habeas Corpus" was also reported in his obituaries. His second wife (Sara), his daughter (Regina), his son (Maurice Barton Anderson) of Evansville, Indiana, and five grandchildren (including Regina Ann) survived Anderson.[8] He had worked as an attorney for nearly 50 years.

Back in New York City, influenced by her father's work with immigrant clients, Regina began the community outreach program at the Washington Heights Branch, Family Night at the Library, which became her passion. Regina recalled, "As a child, I would hear him going out at midnight or 1 A.M. to defend someone who could not speak the language."[9] In her current community, Regina said, "I found that the neighborhood was beginning to slowly change a little bit and people didn't seem to know each other very well." Jews, Germans, and Poles lived in the area, and they learned about other countries as well as about their own.[10]

Family Night was a "library sponsored community forum organized primarily for adults, [which] invites audience participation from all adults— young and old. A variety of themes, presented through speakers, panel discussions, and books, have been concerned mainly with the political, social, and cultural life of countries in South East Asia, Latin America, and Africa. These evenings also function as a meeting place for the many diverse elements of the community engaged in cultural exploration and exchange."[11] Speakers and performers ranged from Arthur Spingarn (head of the NAACP), Lester Granger (executive secretary of the National Urban League), author J. Saunders Redding—"the first African American to hold a full professorship at Brown University"[12]—her old friend Langston

Hughes, and pianist Phillippa Schuyler (who earlier performed at the 115th Street Branch).[13] Family Night programs intersected with Regina's civic interests. She often invited ambassadors that she met as a United Nations (UN) observer representing the National Urban League and the National Council of Women of the United States (NCWUS) to Family Night programs included: Korea—Today and Tomorrow by Ambassador Yong Shik Kim; Red Carpet Reception in the U.S.S.R.; Ghana's Future in the African Framework; Art and Anthropology of Africa; and Regina Woody, author of "Student Dancer" on *The Dance,* with dance interpretations by Ada Fisher Jones, assisted by her pupils. Langston Hughes, accompanied on the piano, also read his poems.[14] Like many of Regina's earlier personal and professional activities, the African American press reported on the Family Night at the Library events held at the Washington Heights Branch.[15]

In 1953, a few years after creating the Family Night at the Library program, Regina became a member of NCWUS and served as vice president in 1963. Regina's mother was also involved with a woman's civic organization decades earlier in Chicago, but while her organization, Necessity Club, focused on helping poor African American women, Regina's organization had an international emphasis on women's issues. Regina held a number of positions in the organization, including cochairman of the Human Relations Committee; chairman of the Education Committee; and Representative of Council at the United Nations. Using her library science skills she compiled a bibliography about intergroup relations when she was cochairman of the Human Relations Committee.[16] The bibliography contained citations to films, organizations, workshops, periodicals, publications, and newspapers. This publication represented Regina's interests in interracial relations and was perhaps an outgrowth of her Family Night at the Library experiences.

NCWUS was an interracial women's organization founded in 1888 by Susan B. Anthony, Clara Barton, Lucy Stone Blackwell, Julia Ward Howe, May Wright Sewell, Elizabeth Cady Stanton, and Frances Williard. The organization's main goal was to provide information about women's issues related to "social, educational and political rights of women."[17] One clue to why Regina would join this organization instead of an African American women's organization might have been the involvement of Sophia Yarnall Jacobs, a white woman, who served as the president of the National Urban League when Regina was a member.[18] Perhaps Jacobs encouraged Regina to join.

Another possible influence on Regina's decision to join NCWUS could be because the organization historically "made an effort to include black women."[19] Decades earlier, Mary McLeod Bethune "felt black women needed an organization to look out for them as the National Council of Women looked out for white females."[20] Mary F. Waring, the National Association of Colored Women's current president, "politely admonished Bethune for what she called 'separatist organizing,' arguing that, contrary to Council member accusations, black women were in fact represented by the predominantly white National Council of Women."[21] Waring had also been the president of the Necessity Club in Chicago when Regina's mother was a member and hosted the first meeting in the Andersons' home.

Membership in NCWUS provided Regina with her first opportunity to travel internationally. In 1958, she was selected to spend four weeks (from mid-April through mid-May) on a study tour to visit eight West German states and/or cities, including Bremen, Bremerhaven, Hamburg, Stuttgart, Berlin, and additional Rhineland cities as a guest of the German Federal government. She was selected by NCWUS "to see how the Marshall Plan had developed."[22] Regina was one of twenty guests, who included ten architects and ten accomplished American women. Regina said, "Germany was my first trip abroad. . . . It was a delightful trip. My first trip overseas in an airplane."

When asked about how she was received in Germany, Regina replied, "It was really beautiful because I don't know, the Germans seemed to make a point of always putting me in the center of everything. I think the Americans were a little [unintelligible] kind of resented that. Why should I be in the center all the time?" Her interviewer, librarian Jean Blackwell Hutson, concluded that there was probably a "racial lack of harmony" on the trip. Further, Hutson remarked, "These people [the Germans] saw you as being an American Negro as a barometer of the state of democracy of the United States. . . . I think you were a symbol."[23] A local newspaper captured part of the visit with a photograph and a caption: "Ten American women who visited Bremen during an informational trip through the Federal Republic of Germany were greeted yesterday morning by government advisers Gisela Muller-Wolff and Heinrich Hilbert." The caption also noted that the women "all have leadership roles in various women's groups."[24] Ironically, although Regina was now a leader as a Supervising Librarian at the Washington Heights Branch, she had to fight over several decades for equal pay and the opportunity to be promoted, both of which were stymied by the racial policies of the organization.

It is not clear who funded Regina's trip to Germany, but scholars such as Mary Dudziak, author of *Cold War, Civil Rights* and Brenda Gayle Plummer, author of *Rising Wind: Black Americans and US Foreign Affairs, 1935–1960*, noted that the U.S. State Department often funded trips abroad for African American citizens to help counter negative international attention about U.S. racial policies. Dudziak wrote, "State Department and American embassy officials recognized that African Americans themselves would be most effective in countering negative international opinion."[25] Dudziak further stated that people "who would say the right thing, from the perspective of the government, could find their travel and international contacts facilitated, directly or indirectly, by the State Department. Talking about progress, and embodying black middle class status, helped reinforce the USIA's message."[26]

The United States was cautious about sending African Americans abroad who might speak out about discrimination in the United States and even revoked the passports of W. E. B. Du Bois and Paul Robeson. The State Department often carefully vetted African Americans before they went abroad.[27] It is not clear whether Regina was among the African Americans scrutinized before traveling abroad. According to the Federal Bureau of Investigation (FBI), she does not have a file.[28] The Central Intelligence Agency (CIA) would "neither confirm nor deny the existence of records" pertaining to Regina.[29]

Regina's trip to Germany placed her squarely in the center of Cold War discussions on the international level. Historian Brenda Gayle Plummer described how unusual it was to discuss African Americans and the Cold War together:

> When I began this work nearly a decade ago, most scholars and, alas, publishers, were puzzled by my coupling of Afro-Americans and foreign affairs. To many, these two subjects seemed to have as little to do with one another as chalk and cheese. [30]

Women's organizations, like NCWUS, were also interested in Cold War politics. Helen Laville wrote in *Cold War Women*, "Even before the end of the Second World War, leaders of American women's organizations were making strenuous efforts to maintain and increase their participation in international relations."[31]

Regina was not a passive representative of the State Department. In 1959, in an interview for the *New York Amsterdam News*, she was critical of the United States and said, "I do think our State Department ought to revise its pamphlet material on the Negro." In reference to the United States trying to reach out to what the reporter called "the darker peoples" of the world, Regina noted that this "has been greatly handicapped by the treatment American Negroes receive at home." She said, "We are developing cultural understanding across the world but before the battle for better understanding is won abroad it must be won at home." Continuing, she stated:

> The U.S. has made a beginning by bringing more Africans here to study but our State Department ought to take more responsibility for all visitors whether

Africans, Asians or Europeans and give them a better opportunity to see all aspects of America. I don't think Mr. Krushchev [sic] got a good view of American Negro life and I fear he probably went back with some misconceptions.[32]

Despite her gentle critiques, several years later Regina would have the opportunity to travel to other continents during her second trip abroad. She enjoyed her trip to Germany and sought additional opportunities to travel internationally. Several years later she would have the opportunity to visit three other continents. In November 1963, Regina sat on the dais with her husband Bill and their daughter Regina Ann, showered with praise, telegrams, and flowers while the Musical Arts Group honored her. Although she was not involved with music, Regina was feted because she had "given generously of her time to broaden the cultural life of all people in the communities in which she has worked and lived."[33]

One honorary member of this organization was Philippa Schuyler, Regina's long-term acquaintance who had been invited by Regina to perform and speak at both the 115th and Washington Heights Branches. In the audience were old Harlem Renaissance friends Langston Hughes and Judge Hubert Delany, Dr. Lester Granger from the Urban League, and Sophia Yarnall Jacobs from NCWUS, as well as the president of the organization, Olive Abbott. The Musical Arts Group awarded Regina an honorarium in the form of an all-expense paid trip to several African nations.[34] "As a woman, interested in serving women's organizations, among others," Regina noted, "I would like to know more of the African woman; of her family life, and of her position in the new frontiers of African civic, political and social life."[35]

On Sunday, February 9, 1964, Regina left JFK International Airport to fly to Lisbon, Portugal. The following day she flew to Dakar, Senegal, and then to Freetown, Sierra Leone, where she stayed for almost two weeks. She visited the University College of Sierra Leone and conducted both radio and television interviews where she spoke about community services provided by public libraries and women's voluntary organizations in the United States.[36]

Regina then flew to Monrovia, Liberia, on February 24th. The next day she arrived for a three-day stay in Accra, Ghana, before traveling to Lagos, Nigeria, for another short stay. From Nigeria, Regina flew to Rome on March 2nd and to Madrid on March 5th, where she departed for Rio de Janerio the next day. She flew to Brazilia, Brazil, and then to the Port of Spain, Trinidad, West Indies, before returning to the United States. She arrived in Miami on March 11th and then flew to New Orleans two days later, finally returning to New York on March 15th. Her trip included eight different carriers: Pan American, BOAC, Ghana Airlines, Italian Airlines, Iberia Airlines of Spain, Varig Airlines, National Airlines, and Delta Airlines; she required five visas for Sierra Leone, Liberia, Ghana, Nigeria, and Brazil. An exhausting trip!

In Lagos, Nigeria, Regina spent an afternoon with the Ladies of the National Council of Women's Societies. In a letter to Lady Adetokunboh Ademola, she described with pleasure "the evening under the stars on your terraced lawn, when we, as dinner and reception guests, heard Chief Magistrate Ademola so warmly address your guest, as he paid tribute to the departing Ambassador."[37] Regina confessed, "We all had such distorted ideas about Africa. . . . It was really one way to learn what you had not learned in books."

While Regina was traveling in West Africa, her daughter and husband were spending time together in New York City. Regina Ann wrote her mother a letter written on letterhead from "The Largest-Selling Fiction-Fact Magazine for Men, Argosy, on East 42nd Street," perhaps where Regina Ann was employed. It was a very jokey letter filled with misspellings: "Work is fine. It couldn't be worse. It's the same things everyday." She noted further, "The house lacks spirit, good carefully made food, the other half of love we share and you. You have no idea how quiet the nights are." They "received all of the telegrams and post cards," she added. "I thought as usual your taste in colors were bright and cheerful. I love the beach scene the best. . . . But those natives in the background have to go. . . . Meanwhile, the natives back here are living, existing and making the best of what ever there is to make the best of." Their friends, the Franks, invited Bill and Regina Ann to dinner, and Regina Ann, "gobbled down the usual Hungarian goulash. Yummy."

Father and daughter also spent a lot of time going to the movies and they saw *Tom Jones*, which Regina Ann liked, and *It's a Mad Mad Mad World*, which she didn't like. They also watched *The Doll*, which she thought "was sick" and "should be banned in the United States as it is in England." She liked *Dr. Strangelove* and really liked *The Manchurian Candidate*. Regina Ann saw *Lilies of the Field* and thought that "Sidney Poitier did a spendid [sic] job." She ended the letter by suggesting possible souvenirs that Regina could bring her, including "a piece of material, or a chipped rock or a (diamond), or a book of recopies [sic], a painting or some ancient or hystorical [sic] tooth, which can be made into a ring or whatever." She also made some stereotypical remarks about Africa when she warned her mother, "if you dare come back speaking one their many tribal languages, and start doing war dances around the house, or start cooking rats eyes, or snakes liver or skunks tails or even olives stuffed with membrane I am shipping you right back there." She signed it "Little Regina Ann" and then informed her mother that she "read this letter to daddy and [he] likes it very much. He feels my style is improving."[38]

Regina returned to her family a little over two weeks after the letter was written. She would later have an opportunity for other adventures abroad.

NCWUS tapped her to represent them on a trip to Asia and the Middle East to attend the All Korean Women's Conference and to visit the Councils in India, Pakistan, Thailand, and "possibly other Asian countries."

NCWUS President Sophia Yarnall Jacobs paid her a compliment:

> Your success last year in Sierra Leone, Nigeria and Ghana in community development and in showing African women how to establish their libraries makes both the Asia Foundation and the Council believe that you are eminently qualified to make a substantial similar contribution in Asia. Its importance in helping stabilize various emerging societies is as obvious as it is urgent. . . . It has long been our feeling that the kind of library program you have conducted [at] the Washington Heights Branch can well serve as a model of the best we have to recommend in promoting good community relations.[39]

While Regina enjoyed traveling internationally and reported being received warmly, her civic activities were sometimes at odds with her work responsibilities as a Supervising Librarian. Regina received a negative response from NYPL administrator Jean Godfrey to her request for additional time off:

> While I am happy for you at the invitation I am sure you realize that I cannot welcome the implications it has for the Library. . . . I am not well disposed to a leave without pay in the light of the other opportunities that you have had of this nature in recent years and because of the Library's leave regulations. . . . In view of the opportunities involved you may wish to accelerate your retirement date so that you will be completely free to take full advantage of the trip and any additional opportunities.[40]

There is no record of Regina's response to Godfrey, but she did travel to Asia and she did not retire until a few years later. In 1965, as the vice president of NCWUS Regina did receive the Asia Foundation Award to travel to South Korea, Japan, India, Pakistan, Afghanistan, Thailand, and Iran. Regina left the United States from San Francisco for the start of her six-week journey.[41]

Although her trips were ostensibly funded by the Asia Foundation and the Musical Arts Group, as mentioned earlier, sometimes international trips were indirectly funded by the State Department; Brenda Gayle Plummer wrote, "Part of the United States' self-presentation involved State Department–subsidized junkets for representative Afro-Americans to Asia and Africa."[42]

This trip was an all-expenses paid award. The Asian Foundation made the hotel arrangements, and Regina had a driver in every country. She reflected, "I'll never forget China and Japan. It was really fascinating to be there."[43] In Korea, she gave a speech that was described at the beginning of the chapter, and the library system also held a reception for her. Later, Regina would give gently used discarded books to Korean libraries. They requested books about U.S. history, fiction, and travel. In India she stayed in the home of Chester Bowles, the U.S. ambassador to India. Regina remembered that during her international travels, "They presented me with a number of gifts in all these countries—China and Japan—beautiful robes that women wear. Lovely things in Korea."[44]

Throughout her tour of various Asian countries, Regina concentrated on meeting women and hearing about the social, educational, and economic issues and concerns that impacted their lives. She also visited libraries and discussed the work that she was doing for both NCWUS and the community programs sponsored by her Washington Heights Branch. This was a perfect opportunity for Regina to make a bigger, international impact as her library career was drawing to a reluctant close.

Both Bill and Regina were reaching retirement age, but nothing was slowing them down. Bill's political ambitions continued, and he became "the first Negro to be named to a city-wide" ticket when he ran unsuccessfully for comptroller.[45]

Not surprisingly, Regina's greatest concern as she approached retirement was the future of her Family Night at the Library program. On May 2, 1966, she wrote Katherine O'Brien, coordinator of the Office of Adult Services for the NYPL, expressing her interest in being able through O'Brien's department to continue to organize the program on a part-time basis.[46] Making valid points, but writing in a condescending tone, O'Brien replied:

> I know of the fine programs you have planned and produced over the years, and I recognize their value to a wide community of readers. I myself have enjoyed many of them although I often found them too long. . . . I do not think it would be professionally wise for you to continue Family Night as a volunteer at Washington Heights Branch. Your successor will have his (or her) own plans, ideas, etc., and will develop them in his own way after he has become acquainted with the community and its needs. . . . Enjoy some new leisure.[47]

Family Night at the Library ended when Regina left.[48] The New York Public Library had a mandatory retirement policy requiring Regina to retire at the age of sixty-five in 1966 after over four decades of service. There is no doubt that she was not ready to quit, and she lived for several decades after her retirement. Regina remained active and continued her involvement with civic organizations. Her interest in international relations never waned. In 1975, nearly a decade after her retirement, Regina rejoined NCWUS.[49] In 1980, she hosted sixty international guests in her retirement community in Lake Mahopac, New York. Regina was able to get local town officials, the Girl Scouts, and the high-school band to participate in welcoming the visitors.[50]

8. Mahopac, New York

Endings

"Last night . . . was free from gunshots," Regina wrote in her own hand as an addendum to her typewritten letter to her friends Mr. and Mrs. J. Newton Hill, representing the African-American Institute in Lagos, Nigeria. She meant to reassure them after typing the following message:

> Events in New York and in Harlem in particular are rather disturbing at present—and apparently growing steadily worse. Rapport between City officials and the man in the streets in Harlem seems to have worsened rapidly since the Republican Convention, as if a foreboding was generated during the Convention days which has cast a shadow even over those who remain aloof and apart. A few incidents in the area of my Library have caused more than a few to pause and think or remain indoors in the evening. . . . [T]he street incidents of the last night were not as serious as heretofore—however, there was no sleep after 3 A.M., when the barking of angry dogs, of police cars and fire engines could be clearly heard from 145th and Lenox to where we live on the roof of 409 Edgecombe.

Regina was referring to the July 1964 Harlem–Bedford Stuyvesant uprising or riot, which was ignited by the shooting death of a fifteen-year-old African American high-school student, James Powell, by an off-duty white police officer, Lieutenant Thomas Gilligan, who was later cleared of any wrong doing. The unrest went on for several days, resulting in the loss of another life and great property damage. Powell was attending summer school along with a number of African American and Puerto Rican students in a predominantly white section of the Upper East Side of New York City. A superintendent of one of the apartment buildings shooed the students away from a stoop with a water hose. The altercation between the superintendent and the students ended with Lt. Gilligan shooting Powell in the back several times.[1]

In the same letter to the Hills, Regina remarked, "We look forward to each weekend's retreat to Lake Mahopac, not as a hiding place, but one giving release from our own frustration." Lake Mahopac provided a refuge from the noise and violence of the city. The Andrewses, who initially purchased this home in the early 1940s as a weekend's retreat, eventually made this property their retirement home. Retirement did not prevent Regina from continuing her participation in civic activities both in Mahopac and in New York City. In fact, Regina was involved with the controversial Harlem on My Mind exhibition at the Metropolitan Museum of Art in New York City.[2]

Perhaps Regina and Bill caught a train from Mahopac to New York City in January 1969 to attend the opening of the exhibit. Maybe they stayed with friends or rented a hotel room and went out for dinner before or after the opening. Whatever the circumstances, attending the exhibition was no doubt uncomfortable due to the protestors outside of the museum.

Regina was invited to become a member of a three-person research advisory panel to consult on the exhibition. The panel included noted historian John Henrik Clarke and Jean Blackwell Hutson, a curator at the Schomburg Center for Research in Black Culture.[3] Susan Cahan said, "*Harlem on My Mind* became one of the greatest fiascoes in the history of American museums. Harlem-based scholars and community leaders felt exploited and misrepresented by the museum. . . . The Harlem Cultural Council withdrew its endorsement of the show." Cahan wrote, "Throughout the exhibition planning process, Schoener, his staff, and his advisors were forced to grapple with serious issues of representation, authenticity, and authority."[4] The advisors, including Regina, were quite sympathetic to the artists and urged the curator, Allon Schoener, to consider the criticism that the exhibition was creating. Later, Schoener admitted that he just wanted the research committee to rubber-stamp his suggestions because he "had little intention of listening to the advice of the research committee members. He now openly admits that he did not want any interference with his vision, even though the idea of creating the advisory board had been his own."[5]

Harlem artists thought that they would finally be able to have their work displayed in one of the greatest museums in the country. However, Schoener decided to create a historical timeline of photographs instead because his "vision was that the exhibition would *only* present documentary photoreproduction and texts, not works of art."[6] In addition to the controversy about the plans for the exhibit, a catalog for the event contained what many declared to be an anti-Semitic essay written by a Theodore Roosevelt High School student, Candice Van Ellison. The essay was based upon a high-school term paper and contained such statements as "Anti-Jewish feeling is a natural result of the black Northern migration." And later, "The lack of competition in this area allows the already badly exploited Black to be further exploited by Jews." New York City's Mayor John Lindsay, the Jewish Defense League, and the American Jewish Congress all condemned the catalog based upon the inclusion of the essay. A disclaimer was placed in the catalog. The New York City Council "threatened to withhold city funds to the Met unless it stopped selling the catalog."[7]

The research advisory panel, including Regina, eventually "withdrew their support for the exhibition on November 22, 1968.[8] Ironically, no other Harlem resident was asked to contribute an essay to the catalog. Scholar Bridget R. Cooks compellingly writes about reaction of the African American community, particularly artists, including Romare Bearden, who actively protested the exhibition and tried to institute change at the Met.

The exhibition opened in January 1969 to "an explosion of protests."[9] Because of the protests, the exhibit never traveled to other museums. Cooks reported, "Despite protests against the Met, thousands of people went to see *Harlem on My Mind*. Ten thousand visited the exhibition on opening day, double the number of visitors on past opening days. An estimated fifteen hundred of those visitors were Black, six to seven times the average daily number of Black visitors to the museum."[10]

One positive outcome of the show for Regina was that she and Clarke were able to create a timeline with photographs; although it did not become part of the exhibition, it later evolved into the publication *The Black New Yorkers*, published posthumously. This was a culmination of a project that Regina worked on for many years. Regina said that her library work had given her an opportunity to learn African American history because none of the schools she attended "except for the short time I was at Wilberforce" ever focused on this aspect of U.S. history. She wanted "to write a book for H.S. and college students."

Although Regina is not listed as one of *The Black New Yorkers* authors, the authors recognized her significant contributions to the publication:

> This book is dedicated to Regina M. Andrews, a pioneer African American librarian. She was also a socially conscious writer, author, civic leader, and activist in the struggle for truth about African American experience. . . . We dedicate this book to her in recognition of her vision, her inspiration, and her commitment to telling the world about the unique and extraordinary role of black New Yorkers in the making of America's greatest city.[11]

Things were more peaceful in Mahopac where Regina dived into community work with the same enthusiasm she exhibited in New York City. She was active in local organizations, greeted visiting foreigners, and hosted famed singer, African American contralto Marian Anderson (no relation). Marian Anderson became well known when, after achieving international acclaim, the Daughters of the American Revolution (DAR) refused to allow her to sing in Constitution Hall in Washington, D.C., in 1939 because they prohibited performers who were not white. First lady Eleanor Roosevelt invited Anderson to sing on the steps of the Lincoln Memorial on Easter Sunday 1939. She performed before an audience of seventy-five thousand.[12] A photograph from an undated and unidentified newspaper shows Marian Anderson standing behind Regina with her hands clasped around Regina's waist. The caption notes:

> World renowned singer Marian Anderson (rear) expresses an appreciative word to her hostess Regina M. Andrews for a recent party which Mrs. Andrews and her husband, former Assemblyman William T. Andrews, held at the home on Long Pond Rd. in Mahopac, in Miss Anderson's honor.

It is unknown how the two women came to know each other, but they continued a casual correspondence, including the exchange of Christmas cards.

Regina's other activities were reported in local papers much like her earlier coverage in the *New York Amsterdam News*, the *Pittsburgh Courier*, and the *Chicago Defender*. Regina was immersed with Mount Hope Church activities and served as the chairman of the Program Committee and the recording secretary of "Willing Workers" for Mt. Hope United Methodists. She was also involved with the Human Rights Public Meeting of Putnam County in Mahopac and was chairman and planner of the first meeting, which was sponsored by the New York State Commission for Human Rights. She produced an exhibit about Negro-African History and Culture presented at the Mahopac Public Library, the Mahopac High School, and the Greenburgh Library in Greenburgh, New York.[13]

Regina was still actively involved with civic organizations in New York City. In 1975, she was a member of the library committee for the National Urban League.[14] As mentioned in Chapter 7, she rejoined the National Council of Women of the United States (NCWUS),[15] and in 1980 she hosted sixty international guests for the NCWUS's International Hospitality Committee in Mahopac.[16]

During this time in Mahopac, the Andrewses' household included a third person—Regina's maternal Aunt Kathreen or Aunt Kate, who lived with Regina when she was a little girl in Chicago. Aunt Kate lived with Regina and Bill until she was one hundred years old, when it became necessary to place her in a retirement home. A local newspaper published an article about Aunt Kate titled, "She's 103 Today—or Tomorrow."[17] The title refers to a light-hearted dispute between Regina and Aunt Kate about when she was born. Aunt Kate insisted it was on Christmas Day, but Regina argued that an old family bible indicated that she was born on December 26, 1876. The reporter described Kathreen Simons as "spirited and mentally alert" and noted that Simons "gets around with a walker and is in otherwise good shape, according to her niece and people at the nursing home." Aunt Kate got out of bed every day and read the newspaper without glasses and enjoyed watching television and listening to music—not surprising since she was a former concert pianist and a music teacher at Methodist and Presbyterian mission schools in Alabama, Arkansas, Arizona, and Mississippi.

Besides being unable to adequately care for Aunt Kate at home, eventually Bill and Regina needed assistance of their own as they aged. For whatever reasons, they did not ask their daughter Regina Ann for help. Regina Ann appeared to have her hands full with her children and her own financial and health problems. In 1984, Regina asked her beloved niece, Margaret (Lorelei), who was living in California to come help her. Lorelei did not think that she could be useful, claiming that she was "not really good at taking care of elderly people."[18] Instead, she sent her daughter, Angelina, who had met Bill and Regina in 1981, during a visit to New York City to attend a conference for work. Angelina had made a two-day trip to Mahopac to meet her great-aunt and great-uncle for the first time. Angelina remembered that Bill liked watching football with her but cautioned against shouting during the football game.[19]

Regina sent a plane ticket, and Angelina stayed for five to six months during her second visit. Bill was quite ill, and Aunt Kate was still living in the nursing home. Angelina also had a chance to meet Aunt Kate, whom she remembered as "a cute little lady" who liked chocolate.

Unfortunately, it appeared that an interloper was prepared to take advantage of the aged couple. Upon her arrival in Mahopac, Angelina found an unrelated woman living with her aunt and uncle for unknown reasons. Regina had met this woman in town and the woman proceeded to "help" Regina spend her money and eventually moved in. Angelina described the woman as "[a] leech. She was a very evil treacherous woman and she saw Aunt Regina as prey." Angelina eventually was able to remove the woman from the household.

Angelina enjoyed her visit with Aunt Regina and Uncle Bill. She said her Aunt Regina "was a fun loving person" who "enjoyed the presentation of her morning breakfast of a complete table setting the china" that Regina's mother had painted. Regina's favorite breakfast was poached eggs, and she showed her grand-niece how to prepare them and how to set a formal table. Although Regina was in her eighties, Angelina said that she was always dressed well and enjoyed Angelina styling her hair and giving her manicures and pedicures.

Regina suggested that one reason for her long life was her daily drink of Jim Beam with a little lemon at high noon. Regina insisted that the drink "stimulated her blood and kept her heart pumping and it kept her healthy," according to her niece Angelina. She also smoked and had a habit of walking around with a lit cigarette but never dropped an ash on the floor.

Although daughter Regina Ann was not able to stay with her parents, Angelina did pick her up with a used car that Regina purchased for her for $500. Regina Ann was living in a not-so-nice neighborhood in the Bronx where she resided with her husband and four children: Kim, Erica, Louis Trent, and Robin. Regina Ann's son's middle name, Trent, was the same middle name as his maternal grandfather and great-grandfather.

In the early 1980s, disturbing letters from Regina Ann suggested financial struggles, medical issues (perhaps more mental than physical), and a continuing fear of being judged for writing ungrammatical letters with misspellings. The passive-aggressive letters often alluded to financial troubles and general unhappiness.

In an undated letter Regina Ann wrote:

> Today my medication has been reduced, not much, but I am happy 'cause I don't take so much. I saw Dr. Polin this morning, and nothing was solved (as usual). But I know for sure and that is I feel more of an individual and I can't stand not telling all about it. I also feel a great amount of love than before too. I know for sure I love you so much. . . . I hope you have a pleasant Easter. Mine won't be too happy but soon I'll be home. I think I better sign off because my eyes are playing tricks. I see double (?) the medication makes things difficult. I love you Mom and Dad—so very much, so very much—Keep well, don't let anything happen to you.[20]

Regina Ann dictated the following letter to her daughter Kim since "her handwriting is more legible than mine":

> All the children and I are still coughing and sneezing from this bug going around. She's [Kim] doing well in school and is making good grades. Erica and Robin are doing well, and Louis Trent is doing exceeding well. His behavior is almost normal compared to last year. Robin will turn 13 next week, and were planning a small get together. Financially, everything's a disaster. I have

mastered knitting and crocheting, some of the neighbors are paying me $5 to knit their children leg warmers, It takes a lot of time away from the children.[21]

Two months later in another letter, Regina Ann wrote:

Please don't be angry with me for not calling you. So much is going on with my life right now. One thing is for sure, I am working as a waitress from 9–10 pm so its [sic] hard to call you in the evenings. So much more, but I'll write you a longer letter after Christmas and explain everything. The children are fine, Kim turns 16 years old on the 20th, and Louis Trent will be getting his school pictures after Christmas vacation. I hope you and Daddy are alright. I know the house is beautiful (as usual) with Christmas decorations all over.[22]

When Angelina drove Regina Ann from the Bronx to Mahopac, she took Regina Ann to visit her father who was now in a hospital and was ailing. After nearly fifty-eight years of marriage, Regina was widowed in 1984 at the age of eighty-three. Bill was eighty-six when he died at the Putnam Community Hospital after a recent move from Tarrytown's Phelps Memorial Hospital. Bill had apparently been ill for some time.

Although second marriages were common in her family, Regina only married once, and she said that they "were very happy."[23] Bill's obituary recalled his work as an attorney and assemblyman and recognized his role as a volunteer in the local Firemen's Association. The memorial service took place at their church, Mt. Hope Church, in Mahopac.[24]

Three years later, more than two hundred people attended a ceremony, including "black scholars, noted writers, musicians, ministers, actors and intellectuals" on a sunny November morning in 1987 at the Schomburg Center for Research in Black Culture located on the corner of 135th Street and Lenox Avenue in Harlem. It was the start of a campaign "to encourage the collection and preservation of black cultural artifacts." Howard Dodson, then chief of Schomburg, made opening remarks, saying, "We're delighted to pick up any and all such items that have a sense of importance to black people in this country and other parts of the world. . . . 'The value assigned to our heritage begins with us.'"[25]

The keynote speaker was singer, actor, and civil rights activist Harry Belafonte. Regina took part in the ceremony dedicated to archiving African American history. She donated her extensive collection of papers, photographs, and books from her and her grandfather Henry Simon's collections. She remarked, "I collected books all my life." The reporter noted that "Mrs. Andrews was merely an observer. Seated under a collection of Marcus Garvey photographs, she said very little." Regina had come full circle. She began her New York Public Library career at the 135th Street Branch, and now her legacy is preserved in the archives collection of the Schomburg Center for Research in Black Culture (the former 135th Street Branch).[26]

Regina lived for nearly a decade as a widow until February 5, 1993, when she died at the age of ninety-one in Ossining, New York, in the Bethel Nursing Home. Regina Ann's daughter, Robyn, recalled that after her Grandfather Bill died, "my family moved to Mahopac NY and my mother took care of her [Regina]."[27]

Regina's death was reported in the *New York Amsterdam News*—the newspaper that had covered her social engagements, creative pursuits, wedding, and professional accomplishments.[28] Reverend Jean Arthur delivered her eulogy, and Regina was buried at the Rosehill Cemetery in Putnam Valley, New York, in an unmarked grave.[29] Her daughter Regina Baptiste survived her.[30] Regina's granddaughter Kimberly recalled almost twenty years after her death that "she was an incredible woman."[31]

On Sunday, May 23, 1993, several months after her death and a few days after what would have been her ninety-second birthday, a memorial service was held for Regina at the location of the first NYPL branch where she worked—the 135th Street Branch—now the Schomburg Center for Research in Black Culture. Several old friends including Dick Campbell and Lofton Mitchell from the theater and Basil Paterson (the father of New York State's fifty-fifth and first African American Governor David Paterson) participated in the program.[32]

A person's last will and testament can be revelatory about who is and is not included. Regina's will was a testimony to her strong commitment to various organizations. Regina did not make her daughter Regina Ann the executor of her estate. Regina appointed Dr. Charles Johnson of Stamford, Connecticut, as the executor. Isabelle Wilmot of Mount Vernon, New York, was to take his place if he could not be the executor.

Regina left several thousand dollars to various organizations located in New York City, including two thousand dollars to the National Urban League and an equal amount to the National Association for the Advancement of the Colored People, one thousand dollars to NCWUS, two thousand dollars to the American Council for Nationalities Services, and one thousand to the Washington Heights Branch of the NYPL. She left her niece Lorelei and her daughter Regina one thousand five hundred and one thousand dollars, respectively. Perhaps this was not the final will because strangely she did not leave any money to her niece Angelina, who helped her when she needed assistance. Regina did exchange correspondence with her namesake Regina,

Lorelei's daughter, and provided her with information about the family tree and photographs.

Regina left additional small amounts to more individuals and then a larger sum, three thousand, to the Mount Hope United Methodist Church in Mahopac. She left the remaining amount to her daughter, Regina Ann, and wanted it distributed as a lump sum of three thousand dollars immediately and one thousand dollars a year, with accrued interest, for twelve years. Conceivably, she considered Regina Ann too irresponsible to adequately manage the funds if she was given it all at once.

Recent contact from one of Regina's granddaughters filled in the history of her daughter Regina Ann's life. After many years of poor health, including suffering a major stroke and several heart attacks, Regina Ann died from lung cancer on January 24, 2006, two days after her sixty-first birthday.[33] Her four children survived her.[34]

Six years before her death when Regina attended the Schomburg ceremony where she donated her papers, the reporter Michel Marriott noted, "About one thing, however, she was emphatic: 'As I have gotten older, I'm glad to have been able to see things get better for the Negro. I'm impressed a great deal,' she said in a firm voice, the feathery fringes of her ample white hair trembling as she spoke. 'I'm very happy.'"[35]

Notes

Introduction

1. Sarah A. Anderson, "'The Place to Go': The 135th Street Branch Library and the Harlem Renaissance," *Library Quarterly* 73, no. 4 (October 2003): 383–421.

2. For the sake of simplicity I use the term *African American* unless I use direct quotes where African Americans are referred to as colored, black, or Negro or when I use commonly used phrases like *New Negro* and *black clubwomen*.

3. Elise Johnson McDougald, "The Task of Negro Womanhood," in *The New Negro: Voices of the Harlem Renaissance*, ed. Alain Locke (New York: Simon and Schuster, 1997), 369–382.

4. Leila G. Rhodes, "Profiles of the Careers of Selected Black Female Librarians," in *The Status of Women in Librarianship: Historical, Sociological, and Economic Issues*, ed. Kathleen Heim (New York: Neal-Schuman Publishers, 1983), 191–205.

5. Steven Ruggles, J. Trent Alexander, Katie Genadek, Ronald Goeken, Matthew B. Schroeder, and Matthew Sobek, *Integrated Public Use Microdata Series: Version 5.0* [Machine-readable database] (Minneapolis: University of Minnesota, 2010).

6. Dorothy B. Porter, "Williams, Edward Christopher," *Africana: The Encyclopedia of the African and African American Experience, Second Edition*, ed. Kwame Anthony Appiah and Henry Louis Gates Jr., Oxford African American Studies Center, http://www.oxfordaasc.com/article/opr/t0002/e4094 (accessed February 22, 2012).

7. Billie E. Walker, "Daniel Alexander Payne Murray (1852–1925), Forgotten Librarian, Bibliographer, and Historian," *Libraries and Culture* 40 (2005): 25–37.

8. Heidi Ardizzone, *An Illuminated Life: Belle da Costa Greene's Journey from Prejudice to Privilege* (New York: W. W. Norton and Company, 2007).

9. Caleb A. Corkery, "Newsome, Mary Effie Lee," *African American National Biography*, ed. Henry Louis Gates Jr. and Evelyn Brooks Higginbotham, Oxford African American Studies Center, http://www.oxfordaasc.com/article/opr/t0001/e1678 (accessed February 14, 2012).

10. Mary W. Plummer, *Training for Librarianship* (Chicago: American Library Association, 1920).

11. Kathleen Thompson, "Harlem Renaissance," *Black Women in America, Second Edition*, ed. Darlene Clark Hine, Oxford African American Studies Center, http://www.oxfordaasc.com/article/opr/t003/e0178 (accessed February 27, 2012).

12. Elinor Des Verney Sinnette, *Arthur Alfonso Schomburg: Black Bibliophile and Collector, A Biography* (Detroit: The New York Public Library and Wayne State University Press, 1989), 132, 134.

13. George Hutchinson, *In Search of Nella Larsen: A Biography of the Color Line* (Cambridge: Harvard University Press, 2006).

14. Lorraine Elena Roses and Ruth Elizabeth Randolph, *Harlem Renaissance and Beyond: Literary Biographies of 100 Black Women Writers 1900–1945* (Boston: G. K. Hall and Co., 1990).

15. David Levering Lewis, "Harlem Renaissance," *Africana: The Encyclopedia*, http://www.oxfordaasc.com/article/opr/t002/e1806 (accessed February 27, 2012).

16. Hutchinson, *In Search of Nella Larsen*, 139–140. Hutchinson cites "Faculty Meeting, Jan. 26, 1922," memorandum in folder entitled "Faculty Meetings, 1921–1922," Box 12, NYPL LS.

17. Hutchinson, *In Search of Nella Larsen*, 143.

18. Thadious M. Davis, *Nella Larsen: Novelist of the Harlem Renaissance: A Woman's Life Unveiled* (Baton Rouge: Louisiana State University Press, 1994), 151.

19. Avril Johnson Madison and Dorothy Porter Wesley, "Dorothy Burnett Porter Wesley: Enterprising Steward of Black Culture," *Public Historian* 17 (1995): 15–40.

20. Interview by Detrice Bankhead, "Augusta Baker," in *Women of Color in Librarianship: An Oral History*, ed. Kathleen De La Pena McCook (Chicago: American Library Association, 1998), 8–27.

21. Audre Lorde, *Zami: A New Spelling of My Name: A Biomythography* (Watertown, Mass.: Persephone Press, 1982).

22. For an excellent overview of the history of African American education in librarianship, see Rosemary Ruhig Dumont, "The Educating of Black Librarians: An Historical Perspective," *Journal of Education for Library and Information Science* 26 (1986): 233–249.

23. Klaus Musmann, "The Ugly Side of Librarianship: Segregation in Library Services from 1900 to 1950," in *Untold Stories: Civil Rights, Libraries, and Black Librarianship*, ed. John Mark Tucker (Champaign: University of Illinois, 1998), 78–92.

24. Louis Shores, "Public Library Services to Negroes," *Library Journal* 55 (1930): 150–154.

25. Charles Rosenberg, "Blue, Thomas Fountain," *African American National Biography*, ed. Henry Louis Gates Jr. and Evelyn Brooks Higginbotham, Oxford African American Studies Center, http://www.oxfordaasc.com/article/opr/t001/e4867 (accessed February 16, 2012).

26. Ernestine Rose, "Work with Negroes Round Table," *Bulletin of the American Library Association* 16 (1922): 361–366.

27. Louise S. Robbins, *The Dismissal of Miss Ruth Brown* (Norman: University of Oklahoma, 2000).

28. "Deny Library's Staff Will Be a Jim Crow One," *New York Amsterdam News*, October 16, 1937, 4.

29. "The Roving Eye," *Wilson Bulletin for Librarians* 10 (1936): 592–593.

30. http://www.bcala.org/association/mission.htm (accessed September 11, 2013).

31. Interview by Marva DeLoach, "Clara Stanton Jones," in *Women of Color in Librarianship: An Oral History*, ed. Kathleen De La Pena McCook (Chicago: American Library Association, 1998), 28–57.

32. Susan E. Cahan, "Performing Identity and Persuading a Public: The Harlem on My Mind Controversy," *Social Identities* 13 (2007): 425.

33. *Labor Force Characteristics by Race and Ethnicity, 2010*, from the U.S. Department of Labor, U.S. Bureau of Labor Statistics (August 2011) Report 1032.

34. Danny P. Wallace, ed., *ALISE Library and Information Science Education Statistical Report 2010* (Chicago: Association for Library and Information Science Education, 2010), 117 and 133.

Chapter 1. Chicago

1. Nathan Irvin Huggins, *Harlem Renaissance* (New York: Oxford, 1971), 25.

2. Ethel Ray Nance, interview by Anne Allen Shockley, tape recording, San Francisco, November 18, 1970, and Nashville, Tenn., December 23, 1970, Black Oral History Collection, Fisk University, Nashville, 32–33.

3. Ibid.

4. Huggins, *Harlem Renaissance*, 25.

5. Paula Giddings, *When and Where I Enter: The Impact of Black Women on Race and Sex in America* (New York: HarperCollins, 1984), 185.

6. Schomburg Center for Research in Black Culture, Regina Andrews Papers, Biographical Material—Personal, New York, N.Y.

7. Regina Andrews and Jean Blackwell Hutson, *An Interview with Regina Andrews*, Schomburg Center for Research in Black Culture, 1986.

8. *Chicago Daily Tribune*, May 21, 1901.

9. Handwritten note on news article about Margaret Simons.

10. For more information about the role of African Americans during the Columbian Exhibition, see Christopher Robert Reed, *"All the World Is Here!" The Black Presence at White City* (Bloomington: Indiana University Press, 2000).

11. Andrews and Hutson, *An Interview with Regina Andrews*.

12. Alfreda M. Duster to Regina Andrews, February 5, 1980, Regina Andrews Collection, Schomburg Center for Research in Black Culture.

13. 1880 Census record.

14. *St. Paul Appeal*, February 21, 1891, 1.

15. David Levering Lewis interview with Regina Andrews, in Voices from the Renaissance Collection, Schomburg Center for Research in Black Culture.

16. *St. Paul Appeal*, February 21, 1891, 1.

17. Ibid., 1.

18. Ibid., 1.

19. Ibid., 1.

20. Clipping from an unnamed newspaper in the Regina Andrews Papers, Schomburg Center for Research in Black Culture.

21. Both homes still exist.

22. Autobiographical document in Regina Andrews Papers, Schomburg Center for Research in Black Culture.

23. Lewis interview with Regina Andrews.

24. Christopher Robert Reed, *Black Chicago's First Century: Volume 1, 1833–1900* (Columbia: University of Missouri Press, 2005).

25. Duster to Regina Andrews, February 5, 1980.

26. "Questioned Five Days; Admits Murder," *Chicago Daily Tribune*, August 20, 1910, 3.

27. "Chicago Police Gives Colored Man Up to Lynchers," *Chicago Defender*, August 27, 1910, 2.

28. "Steve Green Liberated," *Chicago Defender*, September 24, 1910, 1.

29. "Editorial," *Chicago Defender*, October 8, 1910, 2.

30. "Print of Fingers Dooms Murderer," *Chicago Daily Tribune*, November 11, 1910, 1.

31. Ibid.

32. "Negro Must Hang; Fate of 4 Others in Balance Today," *Chicago Daily Tribune*, February 15, 1912, 1. "Jennings to Die; 4 Other Slayers Hear Fate Today," *Chicago Record-Herald*, February 15, 1912, 1 and 3.

Chapter 2. Normal, Illinois; Chicago; Wilberforce; and Chicago Public Library

1. "Famous Habeas Corpus Attorney Gets Divorce," *Baltimore Afro American*, September 30, 1911.

2. "Mrs. Margaret Anderson Secures a Divorce from Her Husband," *Broad Axe*, September 23, 1911, 1.

3. Lorelei, Maurice's daughter, raised by Margaret Anderson Moore, said her grandmother Margaret would never talk about her divorce.

4. "Joseph Freeman, Author, 67, Dies, Wrote 'Never Call Retreat'—Edited Leftist Periodicals," *New York Times*, August 11, 1965, 35.

5. Back of photograph of Regina Andrews with Adlai Stevenson in Regina Andrews Photograph Collection.

6. Consuelo C. Young, "Preface," *Chicago Defender*, October 29, 1938, 13.

7. Rev. G. H. McDaniel, "The Enterprise Institute," *Chicago Defender*, January 27, 1912.

8. "Removal Announcement," *Chicago Defender*, December 20, 1913.

9. "Mrs. Margaret Anderson Gets Blue Ribbon," *Chicago Defender*, October 2, 1915.

10. Wanda A. Hendricks, *Gender, Race, and Politics in the Midwest: Black Club Women in Illinois* (Bloomington: Indiana University Press, 1998), 25.

11. Anne Meis Knupfer, "If You Can't Push, Pull, If You Can't Pull, Please Get out of the Way": The Phyllis Wheatley Club and Home in Chicago," *Journal of Negro History* 82 (1997): 222.

12. Ibid., 223.

13. Ibid., 221–231.

14. "Personals," *Chicago Defender*, August 12, 1911.

15. Susan Butler, *East to the Dawn: The Life of Amelia Earhart* (Cambridge, Mass.: De Capo Press, 1997), 71.

16. A Google search 12/8/07 found: Author: Unattributed Author Source: *from the pillar erected on the Mount in the Dane John Field, Canterbury, in the "Examiner," May 31, 1829.*

17. Lois Brown, *Encyclopedia of the Harlem Literary Renaissance* (New York: Checkmark Books, 2006), sv "Wilberforce."

18. Wilberforce University Catalogue 1919–1920, esp. 22, 180.

19. Donna Tyler Hollie, "Scarborough, William Sanders," *African American National Biography*, ed. Henry Louis Gates Jr. and Evelyn Brooks Higginbotham, Oxford African American Studies Center, http://www.oxfordaasc.com/article/opr/t0001/e3673 (accessed July 27, 2009). Michele Valerie Ronnick, "Scarborough, William Sanders," *Africana: The Encyclopedia of the African and African American Experience, Second Edition*, ed. Kwame Anthony Appiah and Henry Louis Gates Jr, Oxford African American Studies Center, http://www.oxfordaasc.com/article/opr/t0002/e3484 (accessed July 27, 2009).

20. In 2009, this building still existed and housed the administrative offices of the National Afro-American Museum and Cultural Center.

21. "Staff Member of N.Y. Public Library Says Work Demands Better and Higher Training," *Pittsburgh Courier*, January 1, 1927.

22. Wilberforce University Catalogue 1919–1920, 29.

23. Wilberforce University, Register of Students, 180.

24. This building was being renovated when I visited the campus in the fall 2009 term—ninety years after Regina enrolled. It is one of two original Wilberforce buildings that still exist.

25. Wilberforce University Catalogue 1919–1920, 26 and 32.

26. Kevin Boyle, *Arc of Justice: A Saga of Race, Civil Rights, and Murder in the Jazz Age* (New York: H. Holt, 2004), 72.

27. W. E. Burghardt Du Bois, "The Future of Wilberforce University," *Journal of Negro Education* 9 (1940): 553–570.

28. Frederick A. McGinnis, *A History and an Interpretation of Wilberforce University* (Blanchester, Ohio: The Brown Publishing Co., 1941), 176.

29. "Child's Mind Unbalanced," *Chicago Defender*, August 21, 1920.

30. "Diagnosis Proved False," *Chicago Defender*, August 28, 1920.

31. *Book Bulletin of the Chicago Public Library*, Volume 11, No. 6, June 1921, 85–87.

32. Morag Walsh, email messages to author, January 3, 2008, and July 7, 2008.

33. Fifty-First Annual Report of the Board of Directors of The Chicago Public Library 1922, 28.

34. Ibid., 28–29.

35. For a comprehensive coverage of the origins of the Chicago Public Library, see Gwladys Spencer, *The Chicago Public Library: Origins and Backgrounds* (Chicago: The University of Chicago Press, 1943).

36. Marjorie R. Adkins, Carl Bismarck Roden, and the Chicago Public Library, dissertation submitted to the faculty of the Graduate Library School in candidacy for the degree of Master of Arts, The University of Chicago, June 1979, 2.

37. Adkins et al., dissertation, June 1979.

38. September 12, 1921, Proceedings of the Board of Directors of the Chicago Public Library (from July 12, 1920, to December 26, 1921), Vol. XXIII, 225–227.

39. Ibid., 228.

40. June 12, 1922, Proceedings of the Board of Directors of the Chicago Public Library (from January 9, 1922, to December 24, 1923), Vol. XXIV, 90.

41. Fiftieth Annual Report of the Board of Directors of The Chicago Public Library 1921, 5–6.

42. Ibid., 16.

43. Ibid., 23.

44. Ibid., 24.

45. Ibid.

46. October 23, 1922, Proceedings of the Board of Directors of the Chicago Public Library (from January 9, 1922, to December 24, 1923), Vol. XXIV, 158.

47. Michael Flug, "Harsh, Vivian Gordon," *Black Women in America, Second Edition*, ed. Darlene Clark Hine, Oxford African American Studies Center, http://www.oxfordaasc.com/article/opr/t0003/e0183 (accessed August 13, 2009).

48. Laura Burt, "Vivian Harsh, Adult Education, and the Library's Role as Community Center," *Libraries and the Cultural Record* 44 (2009): 234–255. Consuelo C. Young, Preface, *Chicago Defender*, October 29, 1938. David Michel, "Harsh, Vivian Gordon," *African American National Biography*, ed. Henry Louis Gates Jr. and Evelyn Brooks Higginbotham, Oxford African American Studies Center, http://www.oxfordaasc.com/article/opr/t0001/e2850 (accessed August 13, 2009).

49. Oral history interview with Angelina Turner in January 2009 in Beverly Hills, California.

Chapter 3. Harlem Renaissance Women and 580 St. Nicholas Avenue

1. W. E. B. Du Bois to Ernestine Rose, March 1, 1930, Regina Andrews Papers, Schomburg Center for Research in Black Culture.

2. Regina Andrews and Jean Blackwell Hutson, *An Interview with Regina Andrews*, Schomburg Center for Research in Black Culture, 1986.

3. Kathleen M. Rassuli and Stanley C. Hollander, "Revolving, Not Revolutionary Books: The History of Rental Libraries until 1960," *Journal of Macromarketing* 21 (2001): 127.

4. S. G. Fitzgerald, "Home to the Y.," *American Legacy: The Magazine of African American History and Culture* 8 (2002): 59–68.

5. Wil Haygood, *Sweet Thunder: The Life and Times of Sugar Ray Robinson* (New York: Knopf, 2009), 23.

6. Ethel Ray Nance, interview by David Taylor, May 25, 1974, Minnesota Historical Society, St. Paul, 22–23.

7. Steven Ruggles, J. Trent Alexander, Katie Genadek, Ronald Goeken, Matthew B. Schroeder, and Matthew Sobek, *Integrated Public Use Microdata Series: Version 5.0* [Machine-readable database] (Minneapolis: University of Minnesota, 2010).

8. Isabel Wilkerson, *The Warmth of Other Suns: The Epic Story of America's Great Migration* (New York: Random House, 2010).

9. Jonathan Gill, *Harlem* (New York: Grove Press, 2011), 182.

10. Betty L. Jenkins, "A White Librarian in Black Harlem," *Library Quarterly* 60 (1990): 216–231. Celeste Tibbets, "Ernestine Rose and the Origins of the Schomburg Center," Schomburg Center Occasional Papers Series Number Two.

11. Lester A, Walton, "Library Is Barometer of Race's Growth in N.Y.," *Pittsburgh Courier*, August 15, 1925, 6.

12. Committee on Circulation, 1924, 8–9.

13. Ibid., 42.

14. *Bulletin of the New York Public Library—The Director's Report*, 1924, 276.

15. Ibid., 278.

16. Ibid., 291.

17. Thelma E. Berlack, "Chatter and Chimes," *Pittsburgh Courier*, November 8, 1924, 14.

18. Jeffrey B. Ferguson, *The Sage of Sugar Hill* (New Haven: Yale University Press, 2005).

19. Theophilus Lewis, *Messenger*, December 1924.

20. "Harlem Community Forum," *New York Amsterdam News*, June 13, 1923, 12.

21. "Race Superiority Bunk, Says Boas," *New York Amsterdam News*, January 31, 1923, 1.

22. Theophilus Lewis, *Messenger*, December 1924.

23. Regina Anderson to Joseph Freeman, February 13, 1925, Joseph Freeman Papers, Stanford University Hoover Institution Archives.

24. Regina Anderson to Joseph Freeman, March 26, 1925, Joseph Freeman Papers, Stanford University Hoover Institution Archives.

25. "French West African's Opinion of American Negroes Not Flattering," *New York Amsterdam News*, April 4, 1925, 1. "Birth Control Advocate Speaks to Large Audience at Public Library," *New York Amsterdam News*, March 7, 1923, 1. Jeffrey Babcock Perry, *Hubert Harrison: The Voice of Harlem Radicalism, 1883–1918* (New York: Columbia University Press, 2009). "135th St. Library Notes," *New York Amsterdam News*, January

31, 1923, 12, and April 18, 1923, 9. "Library Notes," *New York Amsterdam News*, June 6, 1923, 6, and March 11, 1925, 9. "Library Notes," *Chicago Defender*, November 8, 1924, A8. "Labor Leaders to Address Forum," *New York Amsterdam News*, February 18, 1925.

26. Ethel Ray Nance, interview by David Taylor, 31.

27. Elinor Des Verney Sinnette, *Arthur Alfonso Schomburg: Black Bibliophile and Collector, A Biography* (Detroit: The New York Public Library and Wayne State University Press, 1989), 132, 134.

28. Ethel Ray Nance, interview by Anne Allen Shockley, tape recording, San Francisco, November 18, 1970, and Nashville, Tenn., December 23, 1970, Black Oral History Collection, Fisk University, Nashville, 14.

29. Langston Hughes, "My Early Days in Harlem," *Freedomways* 3 (1963): 312.

30. Ethel Ray Nance, interview by Anne Allen Shockley, 9.

31. David Levering Lewis, *When Harlem Was in Vogue* (New York: Penguin, 1997), 127.

32. Carl Van Vechten, *Nigger Heaven* (Urbana: University of Illinois Press, 2000), 40.

33. Ibid., 40–41.

34. Ibid., 41–42.

35. Ethel Ray Nance, interview by Anne Allen Shockley, 27.

36. Ibid.

37. Ibid., 52.

38. Charles C. Hardy, "Ethel Nance, Black Activist Is Dead at 93," *San Francisco Examiner*, July 19, 1992, B-7.

39. Ethel Ray Nance, interview by David Taylor, 29.

40. Ibid.

41. Ethel Ray Nance, interview by Anne Allen Shockley, 7.

42. Lois Brown, *Encyclopedia of the Harlem Literary Renaissance: The Essential Guide to the Lives and Works of the Harlem Renaissance Writers* (New York: Checkmark Books, 2006), sv "Messenger, The."

43. Ethel Ray Nance, interview by Anne Allen Shockley, 28.

44. Ibid., 33.

45. Ibid.

46. Ethel Ray Nance, Eric Walrond, Arna Bontemps, W. E. B. Du Bois, Langston Hughes, Countee Cullen, and Walter White, *A Man Most Himself* (Berkeley: University of California, Bancroft Library, 1922), 16–17.

47. Ibid., 16.

48. The Messenger *Reader: Stories, Poetry, and Essays from* The Messenger *Magazine*, ed. Sondra Kathryn Wilson (New York: Modern Library, 2000).

49. Gene Ulansky, "A Long-Term Relationship," *San Francisco Sun Reporter*, December 5, 1990, 1.

50. Ethel Ray Nance, interview by Anne Allen Shockley, 21.

51. Ibid., 8.

52. Ethel Ray Nance, interview by David Taylor, 34–35.

53. Nance et al., *A Man Most Himself*, 17.

54. Ibid., 18.

55. Ibid., 17–18.

56. *Encyclopedia of the Harlem Renaissance*, ed. Cary D. Wintz and Paul Finkelman (New York: Routledge, 2004), sv "Ethel Ray Nance."

57. Ethel Ray Nance, interview by Anne Allen Shockley, 48.

58. Ethel Ray Nance, interview by David Taylor, 33.

59. Nance et al., *A Man Most Himself*, 16–18.

60. Ibid., 18.

61. Ethel Ray Nance, interview by Anne Allen Shockley, 33.

62. Van Vechten's literary executor, Bruce Kellner, provided conflicting evidence. In one instance he recalls, "The heroine, Van Vechten told me, was patterned after Dorothy Peterson, the beautiful West Indian girl who worked in the Harlem Branch of the New York Public Library." *"Keep A-inchin Along," Selected Writings of Carl Van Vechten about Black Art and Letters*, ed. Bruce Kellner (Westport, Conn.: Greenwood Press, 1979), 73. Peterson never worked at the Harlem Branch, nor was she West Indian. Peterson was a language arts (French and Spanish) teacher in the Brooklyn school system. Her father was born in New York City, and the family's roots in New York City run deep according to a recent book published by one of Peterson's relatives. Carla L. Peterson, *Black Gotham: A Family History of African Americans in Nineteenth Century New York City* (New Haven: Yale University Press, 2011). In another publication, Kellner stated that, regarding Peterson, "Many friends recognized her as the model for Van Vechten's heroine in his Harlem novel *Nigger Heaven*, a beautiful and cultured woman intensely interested in her racial heritage." *The Harlem Renaissance: A Historical Dictionary for the Era*, ed. Bruce Kellner (Westport, Conn.: Greenwood Press, 281–282), sv "Peterson, Dorothy [Randolph]." This description not only fit Peterson but also matched Regina and most of her Harlem female friends.

63. Van Vechten, *Nigger Heaven*, 42.

64. Ibid., 111–112.

65. Ibid., 42.

66. Lewis, *When Harlem Was in Vogue*, 127.

67. Valerie Boyd, *Wrapped in Rainbows: The Life of Zora Neale Hurston* (New York: Scribner, 2003).

68. Ethel Ray Nance, interview by Anne Allen Shockley, 11.

69. Ibid., 39–49.

70. Ibid., 10.

71. Ibid., 16.

72. Ibid., 16–17.

73. Ibid., 53. In one of the more infamous weddings of the Harlem Renaissance, Cullen married Du Bois's daughter Yolande. Regina hosted a breakfast for the bridesmaids in her Edgecombe Avenue home. "Society—Du Bois Festivities," *Afro-American*, April 14, 1928, 4, col. 5. Cullen was rumored to be gay, and he went to Paris immediately after his wedding not with his new bride (who did join him later), but with his best man, actor Harold Jackman.

74. Kirkland C. Jones, *Renaissance Man from Louisiana: A Biography of Arna Wendell Bontemps* (Westport, Conn.: Greenwood Press, 1992). Arna Wendell Bontemps, *Arna Bontemps—Langston Hughes Letters, 1925-1967,* ed. Charles H. Nichols (New York: Dodd, Mead, 1980).

75. Bontemps, *Arna Bontemps—Langston Hughes Letters,* 445.

76. Ethel Ray Nance, interview by Anne Allen Shockley, 51.

77. Carl Van Vechten, *The Splendid Drunken Twenties: Selections from the Daybooks, 1922-1930,* ed. Bruce Kellner (Chicago: University of Illinois Press, 2003).

78. Ethel Ray Nance, interview by Anne Allen Shockley, 10.

79. Van Vechten, *Nigger Heaven,* 43.

80. Ethel Ray Nance, interview by Anne Allen Shockley, 51–52.

81. Ibid., 32.

82. Ibid.

83. Michael A. Lerner, *Dry Manhattan: Prohibition in New York City* (Cambridge: Harvard University Press, 2007), 201.

84. From WPA Federal Writers' Project Collection, Dorothy West, "Cocktail Party: Personal Experience," 1939, in Lerner's *Dry Manhattan,* 209.

85. Lerner, *Dry Manhattan,* 209, 223.

86. "All Colored Harlem at Walker Wedding—9,000 Invitations Sent," *New York Times,* November 25, 1923, 18.

87. Ethel Ray Nance, interview by Anne Allen Shockley, 50.

88. Ibid., 12.

89. Ibid., 54.

90. Ibid., 31.

91. Brown, *Encyclopedia of the Harlem Literary Renaissance,* s v "Boni & Liveright Publishers."

92. "Society News," *New York Amsterdam News,* September 19, 1923, 8.

93. Ethel Ray Nance, interview by Anne Allen Shockley, 20.

94. Ibid., 21.

95. Ibid., 40.

96. Ibid., 12.

97. Ibid.

98. Sarah L. Delany, A. Elizabeth Delany, and Amy Hill Hearth, *Having Our Say: The Delany Sisters' First 100 Years* (New York: Dell, 1993).

99. Ethel Ray Nance, interview by Anne Allen Shockley, 32–33.

100. Van Vechten and Pfeiffer, Introduction, *Nigger Heaven,* xxvi–xxvii.

101. Ibid.

102. Langston Hughes to Ethel Ray Williams, April 18, 1932, in *A Man Most Himself.*

103. Ethel Ray Nance, interview by Anne Allen Shockley, 32–33.

Chapter 4. Marriage

1. Ethel Ray Nance, interview by Anne Allen Shockley, tape recording, San Francisco, November 18, 1970, and Nashville, Tenn., December 23, 1970, Black Oral History Collection, Fisk University, Nashville, 34.

2. Carl Van Vechten, *Nigger Heaven* (Urbana: University of Illinois Press, 2000), 136.

3. Regina Anderson to Joseph Freeman, n.d., Joseph Freeman Papers, Stanford University Hoover Institution Archives.

4. Regina Anderson to Joseph Freeman (n.d.—Tuesday), Joseph Freeman Papers, Stanford University Hoover Institution Archives.

5. Alexander O. Taylor, "The Buckeye State—Cleveland News—Cleveland Society," *Chicago Defender*, September 13, 1924, 16, col. 1.

6. A. St. George Richardson, "Topic XXII. What Is the Negro Teacher Doing in the Matter of Uplifting His Race?" in *Twentieth Century Negro Literature or a Cyclopedia of Thought Vital Topics Relating to the American Negro by One Hundred of America's Greatest Negroes*, ed. Daniel W. Culp (Naperville, Ill.: J. L. Nichols and Company, 1902), 330, facing 330, facing 331. "Arthur S. George Richardson," in Frank Lincoln Mather, ed., *Who's Who of the Colored Race: A General Biographical Dictionary of Men and Women of African Descent; Vol. 1* (Chicago: Kessinger Publishing, 1915), 230. G. F. Richings, "Prof. A. St. George Richardson," in *An Album of Negro Educators* (Philadelphia: pub. unknown, 1900), 20. G. F. Richings, Illustration, *Evidences of Progress among Colored People* (Philadelphia: Ferguson, 1903?), 141.

7. Unsigned letter to Reggie, Regina Andrews Papers, Schomburg Center for Research in Black Culture, n.d.

8. Regina Anderson to Joseph Freeman, n.d., Regina Andrews Papers, Schomburg Center for Research in Black Culture.

9. Van Vechten, *Nigger Heaven*, 117.

10. Regina Andrews and Jean Blackwell Hutson, *An Interview with Regina Andrews*, Schomburg Center for Research in Black Culture, 1986.

11. Ibid.

12. Ethel Ray Nance, interview by Anne Allen Shockley, 30.

13. *St. Paul Appeal*, March 29, 1890.

14. *The American Heritage Dictionary of the English Language* (Boston: Houghton Mifflin, 2007), sv "huckster," http://www.credoreference.com/entry/hmdictenglang/huckster (accessed September 24, 2009).

15. Florence Murray, "Negroes Admitted to West Point Military Academy," in *The Negro Handbook, 1946–1947* (New York: Macmillan Company, 1949), 341.

16. Mather, *Who's Who of the Colored Race*.

17. Thadious M. Davis, *Nella Larsen: Novelist of the Harlem Renaissance: A Woman's Life Unveiled* (Baton Rouge: Louisiana State University Press, 1994), 127–128.

18. Andrews and Hutson, *An Interview with Regina Andrews*.

19. William T. Andrews Jr. and Regina M. Anderson, Certificate and Record of Marriage, No. 11317, April 10, 1926, at 1945 Seventh Avenue, Borough of Manhattan, New York.

20. "Society News, Andrews-Anderson Nuptials," "A Page of Interest to Women and the House," *New York Amsterdam News*, April 14, 1926, 4.

21. Ibid.

22. "N.Y. State News—New York City—Miss Anderson Marries," *Chicago Defender*, April 24, 1926, A7.

23. Mrs. H. Binga Dismond, "New York Society," *Pittsburgh Courier*, April 17, 1926, 7.

24. Regina Anderson to Joseph Freeman, February 13, 1925, Joseph Freeman Papers, Stanford University Hoover Institution Archives.

25. Joseph Freeman to Regina Anderson, February 18, 1925, Joseph Freeman Papers, Stanford University Hoover Institution Archives.

26. *Bulletin of the New York Public Library*, Volume 30, 1926, 331.

27. "Library Is Barometer of Race's Growth in N.Y.," *Pittsburgh Courier*, August 15, 1925, 6.

28. *Bulletin of the New York Public Library*, Volume 30, 1926, 329.

29. "Staff Members of N.Y. Public Library Says [*sic*] Work Demands Better and Higher Training," *Pittsburgh Courier*, January 1, 1927, 6.

30. Sewell Chan, "Two Bronx Libraries Are Made Landmarks," *New York Times*, April 14, 2009.

31. *Bulletin of the New York Public Library*, Volume 30, 1924, 277.

32. Ibid., 278.

33. *Bulletin of the New York Public Library*, Volume 30, 1925, 229.

34. 1925 Committee on Circulation, 51.

35. "Staff Members of N.Y. Public Library," *Pittsburgh Courier*, 6.

36. Avril Johnson Madison and Dorothy Porter Wesley, "Dorothy Burnett Porter Wesley: Enterprising Steward of Black Culture," the *Public Historian* 17 (1995): 20.

37. Wayne A. Wiegand, *A Biography of Melvil Dewey: Irrepressible Reformer* (Chicago: American Library Association, 1996).

38. Brady Sloan, email messages to author, September 15, 2006, and September 18, 2006.

39. Columbia University, Directory of Students, 47.

40. Columbia University, *School of Library Service Bulletin*, 343.

41. Ibid., 345.

42. Ray Trautman, "Back to Columbia—The Williamson Regime," in *The History of the School of Library Service* (New York: Columbia University Press, 1954), 36.

43. President's Annual Report, School of Library Service, Director Charles C. Williamson, June 30, 1927, 279.

44. Ibid., 304–305.

45. "Pass Bar Examination," *New York Amsterdam News*, January 12, 1927, 1.

46. Margaret Moore to William T. Andrews Jr., January 18, 1927, Regina Andrews Papers, Schomburg Center for Research in Black Culture.

47. "Atty. Andrews Moves Office," *New York Amsterdam News*, June 19, 1929, 11.

48. "Andrews, William T.," in Frank Lincoln Mather, *Who's Who in Colored America* (New York: Christian E. Burckel and Associates, 1950), 12.

49. "Women [*sic*] Recovers $500 for Assault," *New York Amsterdam News*, December 7, 1927, 5.

50. "Manslaughter Verdict for White," *New York Amsterdam News*, February 1, 1928, 1.

51. "N.A.A.C.P. Calls upon Kings Authorities to Jail Patrolman," *New York Amsterdam News*, September 18, 1929, 1.

52. "Police Department Tries Officer Who Insulted Four of Green Pastures Cast," *Afro-American*, 7, col. 4.

53. "N.Y. Cop Fined for Insult to Green Pastures Cast Members," *Afro-American*, June 27, 1931, 15d, col. 7.

54. S. G. Fitzgerald, "Home to the Y.," *American Legacy: The Magazine of African American History and Culture* 8 (2002): 59–68.

55. William T. Andrews Jr. to Regina Andrews, July 4, 1928, Regina Andrews Papers, Schomburg Center for Research in Black Culture.

56. William T. Andrews Jr. to Regina Andrews, July 8, 1928, Regina Andrews Papers, Schomburg Center for Research in Black Culture.

57. William T. Andrews Jr. to Regina Andrews, July 10, 1928, Regina Andrews Papers, Schomburg Center for Research in Black Culture.

58. William T. Andrews Jr. to Regina Andrews, July 12, 1928, Regina Andrews Papers, Schomburg Center for Research in Black Culture.

59. William T. Andrews Jr. to Regina Andrews, July 13, 1928, Regina Andrews Papers, Schomburg Center for Research in Black Culture.

60. Aberjhani, ed., *Encyclopedia of the Harlem Renaissance* (New York: Checkmark Books, 2003), 85, sv "Delta Sigma Theta Sorority." Paula Giddings, *In Search of Sisterhood: Delta Sigma Theta and the Challenge of the Black Sorority Movement* (New York: HarperCollins, 2002).

61. Gerry, "New York, The Social Whirl, 'Frat Gives formal,'" *Baltimore Afro-American[?]*, March 21, 1931, 7, col. 4.

62. "With the Sororities," *New York Amsterdam News*, August 10, 1927.

63. "With the Sororities," *New York Amsterdam News*, January 23, 1929.

64. "Delta Sigma Theta Sorority Members Plan Unique Education Week Program," *New York Amsterdam News*, May 19, 1934, 4.

Chapter 5. The Harlem Experimental Theatre

1. Sarah A. Anderson, "'The Place to Go': The 135th Street Branch Library and the Harlem Renaissance," *Library Quarterly* 73 (2003): 383–421. Ethel Pitts Walker, "KRIGWA, a Theatre by, for, and about Black People," *Theatre Journal* 40 (1988): 347–356.

2. *Crisis*, 1926, 134.

3. Edward G. Perry, "The New Play," *New York Amsterdam News*, January 13, 1932, 10.

4. "New Theatre Offerings Are Held Up by Actors: Good Work by Negro Actors," *New York Amsterdam News*, April 6, 1932, 7.

5. W. E. B. Du Bois to Ernestine Rose, September 12, 1927, W. E. B. Du Bois Papers, University of Massachusetts—Amherst.

6. Eliza Buckner Marquess to W. E. B. Du Bois, September 6, 1927. W. E. B. Du Bois to Ernestine Rose, September 12, 1927. Eliza Buckner Marquess to W. E. B. Du Bois,

September 26, 1927. W. E. B. Du Bois to Ernestine Rose, September 12, 1927. Ernestine Rose to W. E. B. Du Bois, October 18, 1927, W. E. B. Du Bois Papers, University of Massachusetts—Amherst.

7. Loften Mitchell, *Voices of the Black Theatre* (Clifton, N.J.: J. T. White, 1975), 69.

8. Ibid., 73.

9. Amy Helene Kirschke, *Aaron Douglas: Art, Race, and the Harlem Renaissance* (Jackson: University of Mississippi, 1995).

10. Mitchell, *Voices of the Black Theatre*, 73.

11. Ibid., 74.

12. Lois Brown, *Encyclopedia of the Harlem Literary Renaissance* (New York: Checkmark Books, 2006), sv "Paul Green," 198–199.

13. Adrienne C. Macki, "(Re)constructing Community and Identity: Harlem Experimental Theatre and Social Protest," *Journal of American Drama and Theatre* 20 (2008): 107–139.

14. Regina Andrews, "Three Years with the Harlem Experimental Theatre—Its Purpose," *New York Age*, April 11, 1931, 6.

15. "The Community Theater: A Part of the Life of the People," Radio Speech by Regina Andrews, Station WEVD, Friday, September 14, 1934, 10:00 P.M. in Regina Andrews Papers, Schomburg Center for Research in Black Culture.

16. Jay Plum, "Rose McClendon and the Black Units of the Federal Theatre Project: A Lost Contribution," *Theatre Survey* 33 (1992): 144–153. Aberjhani, ed., *Encyclopedia of the Harlem Renaissance* (New York: Checkmark Books, 2003), 211–212, sv "Rose McClendon."

17. "Experimental Theatre in Season's Bow Here," *New York Amsterdam News*, March 23, 1932, 7.

18. "The Community Theater," Radio Speech by Regina Andrews.

19. Macki, "(Re)constructing Community and Identity," 121.

20. Ibid.

21. Steven Ruggles, J. Trent Alexander, Katie Genadek, Ronald Goeken, Matthew B. Schroeder, and Matthew Sobek, *Integrated Public Use Microdata Series: Version 5.0* [Machine-readable database] (Minneapolis: University of Minnesota, 2010).

22. Franklin Hopper to Regina Andrews, June 10, 1930, Regina Andrews Papers, Schomburg Center for Research in Black Culture.

23. "Open-Air Libraries for the City's Poor," *New York Times*, April 24, 1910, 8.

24. Cheryl Lynn Greenberg, *"Or Does It Explode?" Black Harlem in the Great Depression* (New York: Oxford University Press, 1991).

25. Theophilus Lewis, "Negro Stage in This Year of Grace 1929," *New York Amsterdam News*, December 18, 1929.

26. "Drama" and "Experimental Theatre Gives Play," *New York Amsterdam News*, February 3, 1930.

27. Brenda Ray Moryck, "Harlem Experimental Theatre Gives 3 Plays," *New York Age*, May 2, 1931, 6.

28. "Experimental Theatre Group Closing Season," *New York Amsterdam News*, June 21, 1933, 7A.

29. "Harlem Experimental Theater Has Closing," *Chicago Defender*, July 1, 1933, 17.

30. Brown, *Encyclopedia*, 445, sv "Ira De Augustine Reid."

31. Cheryl Black, "Thomas, Edna Lewis," *African American National Biography*, ed. Henry Louis Gates Jr. and Evelyn Brooks Higginbotham, *Oxford African American Studies Center*, http://www.oxfordaasc.com/article/opr/t0001/e1783 (accessed November 27, 2010).

32. "Yank Mag Picks Our Hilda Simms Pin-Up," *Chicago Defender*, March 17, 1945, 13.

33. "Experimental Theatre Two Plays," *New York Amsterdam News*, May 28, 1930, 8.

34. Basil Winters, "Players Presented by Helen M. Brooks," *Chicago Defender*, June 7, 1930, 11.

35. Ibid.

36. James V. Hatch and Leo Hamalian, *Lost Plays of the Harlem Renaissance, 1920–1940* (Detroit, Mich.: Wayne State University Press, 1996), 12.

37. Edward G. Perry, "Harlem Little Theaters Offer Fine Dramas," *Chicago Defender*, May 2, 1931, 11.

38. "3 Plays in New York Score Hit," *Chicago Defender*, May 23, 1931, 3.

39. Moryck, "Harlem Experimental Theatre," 6.

40. "3 Plays in New York Score Hit," *Chicago Defender*, 3.

41. I. M. R., "Local Players in Three Plays," *New York Amsterdam News*, April 13, 1932, 7.

42. "'Goat Alley' Is the Next for the East," *Chicago Defender*, April 8, 1933, 5.

43. Tim Brooks, *Lost Sounds: Blacks and the Birth of the Recording Industry, 1890–1919* (Urbana: University of Illinois Press, 2004), 266.

44. Bessye Bearden, "New York Raves as 'Goat Alley' Opens," *Chicago Defender*, April 15, 1933, 5.

45. "Burroughs Play Gets Attention: Experimental Theatre Group Rehearsing Writer's Opus—Other Play Notes," *New York Amsterdam News*, November 25, 1931, 10.

46. Carolyn G. Heilbrun, *Writing a Woman's Life* (New York: Ballantine Books, 1988), 111–112.

47. Kathy A. Perkins, *Black Female Playwrights: An Anthology of Plays before 1950* (Bloomington: Indiana University Press, 1989), 2.

48. Regina M. Anderson to Joseph Freeman, Tuesday [n.d.], Joseph Freeman Papers, Hoover Institute, Stanford University.

49. Katherine Wilson, "Theater Near Us: Librarians, Culture, and Space in the Harlem Renaissance," in *Unmaking Race, Remaking Soul: Transformative Aesthetics and the Practice of Freedom*, ed. Christa Davis Acampora and Angela L. Cotton (Albany: State University of New York Press, 2007), 231–245, 236.

50. Kathy A. Perkins and Judith L. Stephens, eds., *Strange Fruit: Plays on Lynching by American Women* (Bloomington: Indiana University Press, 1998). Koritha Ann Mitchell, "A Different Kind of 'Strange Fruit': Lynching Drama, African American Identity, and U. S. Culture, 1890–1935," PhD dissertation, University of Maryland, College Park. Judith L. Stephens, "Anti-Lynch Plays by African American Women:

Race, Gender, and Social Protest in American Drama," *African American Review* 26 (1992): 329–339.

51. Wilson, "Theater Near Us," 234.

52. Regina Andrews, "Matilda" (unpublished manuscript), Regina Andrews Papers, Schomburg Center for Research in Black Culture.

53. Regina M. Andrews, "The Man Who Passed," in *Harlem's Glory: Black Women Writing 1900–1950*, ed. Elizabeth Randolph Ruth and Lorraine Elena Roses (Cambridge: Harvard University Press, 1996), 45–55.

54. Ethel Ray Nance, interview by Anne Allen Shockley, tape recording, San Francisco, November 18, 1970, and Nashville, Tenn., December 23, 1970, Black Oral History Collection, Fisk University, Nashville, 37.

55. Mitchell, *Voices of the Black Theatre*, 78.

56. Regina M. Andrews, "Climbing Jacob's Ladder," in *Strange Fruit: Plays on Lynching by American Women*, ed. Kathy A. Perkins and Judith L. Stephens (Bloomington: Indiana University Press, 1998), 121–132.

57. Perkins and Stephens, eds., *Strange Fruit*, 9–10.

58. W. E. B. Du Bois to Regina Andrews, Regina, January 27, 1931, Special Collections and Archives, W. E. B. Du Bois Papers, University of Massachusetts—Amherst.

59. W. E. B. Du Bois to Regina Andrews, Regina, Special Collections and Archives, W. E. B. Du Bois Papers, University of Massachusetts—Amherst. Mitchell, *Voices of the Black Theatre*, 79.

60. Moryck, "Harlem Experimental Theatre," 6.

61. Mitchell, "A Different Kind of 'Strange Fruit.'"

62. "The Harlem Experimental Theatre in a Scene from 'Climbing Jacob's Ladder,' An Original Play by Regina Andrews," *Crisis*, July 1931, 236.

63. Joan Cook, "Ella Winter Stewart, Journalist and Widow of Donald O. Stewart," *New York Times*, August 5, 1980, B10.

64. Boris Pil'njak to Joseph Freeman, October 3, 1931, Joseph Freeman Papers, Stanford University Hoover Institute Archives. Letter translated by Elena Tranquilli.

65. Translation from the original Russian by Elena Tranquilli. No English translation of the novel exists.

66. For additional information, see Gary Browning, *Boris Pilniak: Scythian at a Typewriter* (Ann Arbor, Mich.: Ardis, 1985). Vera T. Reck, *Boris Pil'niak: A Soviet Writer in Conflict with the State* (Montreal: McGill, Queen's University Press, 1975).

67. "Experimental Theatre Announces New Plans," *New York Amsterdam News*, September 27, 1933, 7.

68. Brown, *Encyclopedia*, 453, sv "Riding the Goat."

69. "'Home' Leads the Nominations for Awards in Black Theater," *New York Times*, November 17, 1980, 18. "A Kiss for Audelco," *New York Amsterdam News*, November 29, 1980, 29. "Black Theatre's Historians Huddle," *New York Amsterdam News*, November 7, 1981, 26.

70. "Rob AUDELCO: Irreplaceable Black Theatre Files Taken," *New York Amsterdam News*, March 17, 1990, 25.

71. Esther Spring Arata, *More Black American Playwrights: A Bibliography* (Metuchen, N.J.: Scarecrow Press, Inc., 1978). Esther Spring Arata and Nicholas John Rotoli, *Black American Playwrights, 1800 to the Present: A Bibliography* (Metuchen, N.J.: Scarecrow Press, Inc., 1976). Theressa Gunnels Rush, Carol Fairbanks Myers, and Esther Spring Arata, *Black American Writers Past and Present: A Biographical and Bibliographical Dictionary, Vol. 1: A-I* (Metuchen, N.J.: Scarecrow Press, Inc., 1975).

72. Perkins and Stephens, eds., *Strange Fruit*, 22.

Chapter 6. The New York Public Library

1. Sarah A. Anderson, "'The Place to Go': The 135th Street Branch Library and the Harlem Renaissance," *Library Quarterly* 73 (2003): 383–421.

2. Phyllis Dain, *New York Public Library: A History of Its Founding and Early Years* (New York: New York Public Library, 1972).

3. Jessie Carney Smith, ed., *Notable Black American Women* (Detroit: Gale Research, 1992).

4. David Levering Lewis, *W. E. B. Du Bois: The Fight for Equality and the American Century, 1919–1963* (New York: Henry Holt and Company, 2000).

5. Felix L. Armfield, *Eugene Kinckle Jones: The National Urban League and Black Social Work, 1910–1940* (Chicago: University of Illinois Press, 2012).

6. Memorandum, January 11, 1932, W. E. B. Du Bois Papers, University of Massachusetts—Amherst.

7. Catherine A. Latimer to W. E. B. Du Bois, September 7, 1932, W. E. B. Du Bois Papers, University of Massachusetts—Amherst.

8. Catherine A. Latimer to W. E. B. Du Bois, January 29, 1932, W. E. B. Du Bois Papers, University of Massachusetts—Amherst.

9. W. E. B. Du Bois, Memorandum, Regina Andrews Papers, Schomburg Center for Research in Black Culture.

10. W. E. B. Du Bois to Ferdinand Q. Morton, February 18, 1930, *The Correspondence of W. E. B. Du Bois (Volume 1) Selections 1877–1934*, ed. Herbert Aptheker (Amherst: University of Massachusetts Press, 1973), 416–417.

11. W. E. B. Du Bois to Franklin F. Hopper, March 1, 1930, Regina Andrews Papers, Schomburg Center for Research in Black Culture. W. E. B. Du Bois to Ernestine Rose, March 1, 1930, Regina Andrews Papers, Schomburg Center for Research in Black Culture.

12. Kenneth Robert Janken, *White: The Biography of Walter White, Mr. NAACP* (New York: The New Press, 2003).

13. Walter White to Ernestine Rose, February 20, 1930, Regina Andrews Papers, Schomburg Center for Research in Black Culture.

14. Carl Van Vechten, *Nigger Heaven* (Urbana: University of Illinois Press, 2000), 119.

15. Ibid., 30.

16. Franklin F. Hopper to Regina A. Andrews, June 10, 1930, Regina Andrews Papers, Schomburg Center for Research in Black Culture.

17. "New Negro Libraries," *Crisis*, September 1932, 284–285.

18. Regina Andrews to Mr. Faull, July 20, 1936, Regina Andrews Papers, Schomburg Center for Research in Black Culture.

19. Jervis Anderson, *This Was Harlem: A Cultural Portrait, 1900–1950* (New York: Farrar Straus Giroux, 1982), 343.

20. Box 30, f. NYPL BL-Chief of Circulation 1934–1939, Hopper R. Andrews transferred from Rivington Street to 115th Street, 12/1/36.

21. *Bulletin of the New York Public Library*, Volume 41, 1937, Exhibitions, 210.

22. *Bulletin of the New York Public Library*, Volume 43, 1939, 229.

23. *Bulletin of the New York Public Library*, Volume 42, 1938, 219.

24. "Appointed as One of Chief Librarians in Public Library System, New York City," *Pittsburgh Courier*, October 1, 1938, 13.

25. "Opening of Little Theatre and Auditorium," November 3, 1938, Regina Andrews Papers, Schomburg Center for Research in Black Culture.

26. *Public School Bulletin*, Volume 42, 1938, 281.

27. *Public School Bulletin*, Volume 43, 1939, 156.

28. Franklin F. Hopper to To Whom It May Concern, March 31, 1939, Regina Andrews Papers, Schomburg Center for Research in Black Culture. Franklin F. Hopper to Regina A. Andrews, May 28, 1938, Regina Andrews Papers, Schomburg Center for Research in Black Culture.

29. Committee on Circulation Minutes, Meeting of March 3, 1939, 61.

30. Newspaper clipping in Regina Andrews Papers, Schomburg Center for Research in Black Culture.

31. Kathryn Talalay, *Composition in Black and White: The Life of Philippa Schuyler* (New York: Oxford University Press, 1995).

32. Brochure from the Women's Service League of Brooklyn, Regina Andrews Papers, Schomburg Center for Research in Black Culture.

33. Anne Lundin, "Anne Carroll Moore (1871–1961): 'I Have Spun Out a Long Thread,'" in *Reclaiming the American Library Past: Writing the Women*, ed. Suzanne Hildenbrand (Norwood, N.J.: Ablex Publishing Company, 1996), 187–204.

34. Consuelo C. Young, Preface, *Chicago Defender*, October 29, 1938, 13.

35. Julio L. Hernandez-Delgado, "Pura Teresa Belpre, Storyteller and Pioneer Puerto Rican Librarian," *Library Quarterly* 62 (1992): 425–440.

36. Committee on Circulation, 1939, 11 and 204.

37. Hubert T. Delany to Regina Anderson Andrews, September 22, 1938, Regina Andrews Collection, Schomburg Center for Research in Black Culture.

38. "N.A.A.C.P. Drops Attorney Andrews," *New York Amsterdam News*, February 3, 1932, 3.

39. "Andrews to Run for N.Y. Assembly," *Afro-American*, August 4, 1934, 13, col. 2.

40. "Assembly Records Praised in Report," *New York Times*, September 11, 1935, 18.

41. Carl Dunbar Lawrence, "Scramble on for Gavagan's Seat," *New York Amsterdam News*, August 28, 1943, 1.

42. Julius J. Adams, "Political News and Views," *New York Amsterdam News*, November 27, 1943, 7A.

43. Earl Brown, "Timely Topics," *New York Amsterdam News*, February 19, 1944, 6.

44. Ibid. "Andrews Certain He'll Beat Powell for Legislature," *Chicago Defender*, April 15, 1944, 1.

45. "Andrews to Face Stiff Opposition," *New York Amsterdam News*, May 20, 1944, 5A.

46. Ramona Lowe, "Harlem Goes to Roosevelt by 4-to-1 Landslide," *Chicago Defender*, November 18, 1944, 3.

47. Loften Mitchell, *Voices of the Black Theatre* (Clifton, N.J.: J. T. White, 1975), 64.

48. Ibid., 65.

49. Errol G. Hill and James V. Hatch, *A History of African American Theatre* (New York: Cambridge University Press, 2003), 362–363.

50. Elsa Brenner, "Living In/Mahopac, N.Y.: Nature Has Protectors Here," *New York Times*, January 20, 2008.

51. Ibid.

52. Ibid.

53. Franklin F. Hopper to Regina Andrews, February 19, 1940, Regina Andrews Papers, Schomburg Center for Research in Black Culture.

54. Regina M. Andrews, "A Public Library Assists in Improving Race Relations," Thesis, New York Public Library—Circulation Department, 1945, 1.

55. Ibid., 14.

56. Francis R. St. John to Regina Andrews, July 18, 1946, Regina Andrews Papers, Schomburg Center for Research in Black Culture.

57. Francis R. St. John to W. E. B. Du Bois, December 20, 1946, Regina Andrews Papers, Schomburg Center for Research in Black Culture.

58. W. E. B. Du Bois to Francis R. St. John, December 31, 1946, Regina Andrews Papers, Schomburg Center for Research in Black Culture.

59. Laura Ruttum, Manuscripts and Archives, New York Public Library, email message to author, January 21, 2008.

60. Around 1957, in Sophia Yarnall Jacobs's papers, Andrews mentioned that she had an eleven-year-old adopted daughter.

61. Maureen G. Malone, email message to author, November 12, 2007.

62. Robyn Baptiste, email message to author, March 18, 2013.

63. Robyn Baptiste, email message to author, March 20, 2013.

64. Robyn Baptiste, email message to author, March 19, 2013.

65. Regina Andrews, "Family Night at the Library," *Top of the News* 10 (1953): 31.

66. 1925 Washington Heights Branch Annual Report.

67. Regina Andrews Papers, The City of New York, Department of Personnel, Bureau of Classification and Compensation, Position Classification Questionnaire, June 14, 1957.

68. Andrews, "Family Night at the Library," 31.

69. Maureen G. Malone, email message to author, January 21, 2007.

Chapter 7. International Flights

1. Regina M. Andrews to Mrs. Norman Coliver, January 8, 1956, Records of the National Council of Women of the United States, Inc., 1888–ca. 1970.

2. Toure F. Reed, *Not Alms but Opportunity: The Urban League and the Politics of Racial Uplift, 1910–1950* (Chapel Hill: University of North Carolina, 2008).

3. Ed Thomasson, "Mrs. Regina Andrews," *New York Amsterdam News*, December 26, 1959, 7.

4. Alfreda M. Duster to Regina Andrews, February 5, 1980, Regina Andrews Collection, Schomburg Center for Research in Black Culture.

5. Aunt Kate to Regina, July 19, 1948, Regina Andrews Collection, Schomburg Center for Research in Black Culture.

6. "Harlem's First Negro Loan Bank Open," *New York Amsterdam News*, January 8, 1949, 1.

7. "Who's Who in New York? Carver Legal Counsel Is Former Legislator," unknown newspaper, n.d., 1.

8. Obituaries, "William G. Anderson," *Chicago Daily Tribune*, January 9, 1950, A6. "Habeas Corpus Expert Dies," *Chicago Defender*, January 14, 1950, 11.

9. Carolyn Fitzgerald, "Hudson Slaves and Harlem: A Black History of New York," unknown newspaper, n.d., Regina Andrews Papers, Schomburg Center for Research in Black Culture.

10. Regina M. Andrews, "Family Night at the Library," *Top of the News* 10 (1953): 31–33.

11. Resumé, n.d., Regina Andrews Papers, Schomburg Center for Research in Black Culture.

12. Kimberly Welch, "Redding, J. Saunders," *African American National Biography*, ed. Henry Louis Gates Jr. and Evelyn Brooks Higginbotham, *Oxford African American Studies Center*, http://www.oxfordaasc.com/article/opr/t0001/e0789 (accessed November 12, 2010).

13. Andrews, "Family Night at the Library," 31–33.

14. Langston Hughes to Regina Andrews, January 14, 1955, Regina Andrews Papers, Schomburg Center for Research in Black Culture.

15. Melvin Tapley, "Artists Go to Market Too," *New York Amsterdam News*, December 13, 1952, 34. "Dancer to Speak at Heights Library," *New York Amsterdam News*, January 3, 1953, 12. "Family Night One Feature at Libraries," *New York Amsterdam News*, April 25, 1953, 17. "Discuss Women of Ghana at Library," *New York Amsterdam News*, October 29, 1960, 12. "Miss Schuyler African Series Library Speaker," *New York Amsterdam News*, December 10, 1960, 15. "Warning Issued on S. Africa," *New York Amsterdam News*, July 18, 1964, 15. "To Turn Series on New Japan at Library," *New York Amsterdam News*, February 5, 1966, 7. "Photo Standalone 5—No Title," *New York Amsterdam News*, March 5, 1966, 10. "Pakistan Will Be the Topic," *New York Amsterdam News*, May 14, 1966, 24.

16. Regina M. Andrews, *Intergroup Relations in the United States: A Compilation of Source Materials and Service Organizations* (New York: The Human Relations Committee of the National Council of Women of the United States, 1956).

17. Laura K. O'Keefe, Introduction, Records of the National Council of Women of the United States, Inc., 1888–ca. 1970, *A Guide to the Microfiche Edition*, New York Public Library, vii.

18. Marvine Howe, "Sophia Jacobs, 91, in Forefront of Fight For Human Rights," *New York Times*, July 2, 1993, D20.

19. Deborah Gray White, *Too Heavy a Load: Black Women in Defense of Themselves, 1894–1994* (New York: W. W. Norton and Company, 1999), 40.

20. Ibid., 149.

21. Ibid., 156.

22. Regina Andrews CV, Regina Andrews Papers, Schomburg Center for Research in Black Culture.

23. Regina Andrews, *Interview by Jean Blackwell Hutson*, Videorecording, July 16, 1986, New York, Schomburg Center for Research in Black Culture.

24. *Weser Kurier Bremer Tageszeitung* (Bremen Daily Newspaper), Nr. 97, 3.

25. Mary L. Dudziak, *Cold War, Civil Rights: Race and the Image of American Democracy* (Princeton: Princeton University Press, 2000), 56.

26. Ibid., 61.

27. Ibid.

28. U.S. Department of Justice, Federal Bureau of Investigation (David M. Hardy, Section Chief, Record/Information Dissemination Section Records Management Division), letter to author, November 20, 2008.

29. Central Intelligence Agency (Michele Meeks, Information and Privacy Coordinator), letter to author, February 4, 2013.

30. Brenda Gayle Plummer, *Rising Wind: Black Americans and U. S. Foreign Affairs, 1935–1960* (Chapel Hill: University of North Carolina, 1996), 2. Brenda Gayle Plummer, "Peace Was the Glue: Europe and African American Freedom," *Souls: A Critical Journey of Black Politics, Culture and Society* 10: 103–122.

31. Helen Laville, *Cold War Women: The International Activities of American Women's Organizations* (New York: Manchester University Press, 2002), 5.

32. Thomasson, "Mrs. Regina Andrews," 7.

33. Olive Abbott to Vivian Beaman, October 12, 1963, Regina Andrews Papers, Schomburg Center for Research in Black Culture.

34. "Musical Art Group Fetes N.Y.'s Regina Andrews, *New Pittsburgh Courier*, November 30, 1963, 17.

35. A letter of reference for Regina Andrews from Sophia Yarnall Jacobs, Schlesinger Library, Radcliffe, Sophia Yarnall Jacobs Papers.

36. Olive Abbott to Vivian Beaman, October 12, 1963, Regina Andrews Papers, Schomburg Center for Research in Black Culture.

37. Regina M. Andrews to Lady Adetokunboh Ademola, July 29, 1964, Regina Andrews Papers, Schomburg Center for Research in Black Culture.

38. Regina Ann Andrews to Regina Andrews, February 17, 1964, Regina Andrews Papers, Schomburg Center for Research in Black Culture.

39. Sophia Yarnall Jacobs to Regina Andrews, September 2, 1964, Regina Andrews Papers, Schomburg Center for Research in Black Culture.

40. Jean Godfrey to Regina Andrews, September 17, 1964, Regina Andrews Papers, Schomburg Center for Research in Black Culture.

41. Regina M. Andrews to Mrs. Norman Coliver, January 8, 1965, Regina Andrews Papers, Schomburg Center for Research in Black Culture.

42. Plummer, *Rising Wind*, 212.

43. Andrews, *Interview by Jean Blackwell Hutson*, Videorecording. .

44. Ibid.

45. "Andrews Runs with O'Dwyer," *New York Amsterdam News*, July 31, 1965, 3.

46. Regina Andrews to Katherine O'Brien, May 2, 1966, Regina Andrews Papers, Schomburg Center for Research in Black Culture.

47. Katherine L. O'Brien to Regina Andrews, May 16, 1966, Regina Andrews Papers, Schomburg Center for Research in Black Culture.

48. Edward G. Freehafer to Regina Andrews, January 12, 1967, Regina Andrews Papers, Schomburg Center for Research in Black Culture.

49. Dorothea Hopfer to Mrs. Regina M. Andrews, November 25, 1975, Regina Andrews Papers, Schomburg Center for Research in Black Culture.

50. Betti Salzman to Mr. and Mrs. William Andrews, October 6, 1980, Regina Andrews Papers, Schomburg Center for Research in Black Culture.

Chapter 8. Mahopac, New York

1. Janet L. Abu-Lughod, *Race, Space, and Riots in Chicago, New York, and Los Angeles* (New York: Oxford University Press, 2007).

2. Allon Schoener, ed., *Harlem on My Mind: Cultural Capital of Black America 1900–1968* (New York: The New Press, 1968).

3. Ibid., 423–440.

4. Ibid., 428.

5. Ibid., 432.

6. Ibid., 428–429.

7. Bridget R. Cooks, "Black Artists and Activism: Harlem on My Mind (1969)," *American Studies* 48 (2007): 20.

8. Ibid., 18.

9. Susan E. Cahan, "Performing Identity and Persuading a Public: The Harlem on My Mind Controversy," *Social Identities* 13 (2007): 432.

10. Cooks, "Black Artists and Activism," 26.

11. Howard Dodson, Christopher Moore, and Roberta Yancy, *The Black New Yorkers: The Schomburg Illustrated Chronology* (New York: John Wiley and Sons, Inc., 2000).

12. Antoinette Handy, "Anderson, Marian," *African American National Biography*, ed. Henry Louis Gates Jr. and Evelyn Brooks Higginbotham. *Oxford African American Studies Center*, http://www.oxfordaasc.com/article/opr/t0001/e0015 (accessed April 15, 2010).

13. Regina Andrews C.V., Regina Andrews Papers, Schomburg Center for Research in Black Culture.

14. John J. Cardwell Jr. to Mrs. William T. Andrews, May 16, 1975, Regina Andrews Papers, Schomburg Center for Research in Black Culture.

15. Dorothea Hopfer to Mrs. Regina M. Andrews, November 25, 1975, Regina Andrews Papers, Schomburg Center for Research in Black Culture.

16. Betti Salzman to Mr. and Mrs. William Andrews, October 6, 1980, Regina Andrews Papers, Schomburg Center for Research in Black Culture.

17. *Evening Star*, December 25, 1979.

18. Angelina Turner, *Interview by Ethelene Whitmire*, Videorecording, January 2008, Beverly Hills.

19. Ibid.

20. Regina Ann Baptiste to Dearest Mom and Dad, Tuesday, Regina Andrews Papers, Schomburg Center for Research in Black Culture.

21. Regina Ann Baptiste dictated to Kim Baptiste to Dear Mom and Daddy, October 13, 1983, Regina Andrews Papers, Schomburg Center for Research in Black Culture.

22. Regina Ann Baptiste to Hi Mom and Daddy, December 13, 1983, Regina Andrews Papers, Schomburg Center for Research in Black Culture.

23. Regina Andrews and Jean Blackwell Hutson, *An Interview with Regina Andrews*, Schomburg Center for Research in Black Culture, 1986.

24. "William Andrews Was Long Time City Attorney," *New York Amsterdam News*, September 15, 1984, 33.

25. "Regina Andrews Memorial Sunday at Schomburg," *New York Amsterdam News*, May 22, 1993, 32.

26. Michel Marriott, "Schomburg Center Acts to Halt Loss of Black History," *New York Times*, November 23, 1987, B1.

27. Robyn Baptiste, email message to author, September 12, 2011.

28. Herb Boyd, "Regina Andrews Was Noted Activist, Scholar," *New York Amsterdam News*, February 20, 1993, 36.

29. Author's phone call to Rosehill Cemetery in October 2011.

30. Boyd, "Regina Andrews was Noted," 36.

31. Kimberly Andrews, email message to author, September 12, 2011.

32. "Regina Andrews Memorial Sunday at Schomburg," *New York Amsterdam News*, May 22, 1993, 32.

33. Ancestry.com, *U.S., Social Security Death Index, 1935-Current* [database online] (Provo, Utah: Ancestry.com Operations, Inc., 2011).

34. Robyn Baptiste, email message to author, March 22, 2013.

35. Michel Marriott, "Schomburg Center Acts to Halt Loss of Black History," *New York Times*, November 23, 1987, B1.

Index

ETHELENE WHITMIRE is an associate professor of library and information studies at the University of Wisconsin–Madison.

The University of Illinois Press
is a founding member of the
Association of American University Presses.

———————————————————

Composed in 10.5/13 Adobe Minion Pro
at the University of Illinois Press
Manufactured by Thomson-Shore, Inc.

University of Illinois Press
1325 South Oak Street
Champaign, IL 61820-6903
www.press.uillinois.edu